ADVANCE PRAISE FOR *NO REGRETS PARENTING* BY DR. HARLEY ROTBART

"Dr. Rotbart has a gift for uncovering and explaining the countless possibilities in parenting. This book is a treasure for all of us with children."
> —Jeffrey Zaslow, number-one *New York Times* best-selling coauthor of *The Last Lecture*, and *Moving On* columnist for the *Wall Street Journal*

"What's more precious than love, your children, and time? *No Regrets Parenting* is a gem of a book. It will help you turn the minutes of the day into the moments of your life."
> —Harvey Karp, MD, creator of the *New York Times* best-selling books and DVDs *The Happiest Baby on the Block* and *The Happiest Toddler on the Block*

"*No Regrets Parenting* helps today's busy parents stop worrying about trying to be perfect, and offers low-key ways to make the most of the time they spend with their children. Whether you're a working parent or stay-at-home mom or dad, Dr. Rotbart's wise advice and refreshing ideas will make you want to pick up this book again and again."
> —Diane Debrovner, deputy editor of *Parents* magazine

"During the long, hectic days of in-the-trenches parenting, it's easy to forget the all too fleeting nature of childhood. To someday look back on your children's formative years with fond nostalgia—but *No Regrets*—Dr. Rotbart guides you in maximizing and optimizing the time you spend with your kids. *No Regrets Parenting* reminds parents everywhere that the essence of successful parenting is simply *being* there. This book helps you find the time."
> —Marianne Neifert, MD (Dr. Mom®), pediatrician, speaker, and author of the best-selling *Dr. Mom* books for parents

---

"A poignant, timely book to remind us to savor parenting our kids—with awesome tips on how to slow the daily chaos, create memorable moments, and luxuriate in the wonder and fun of each age and stage."
> —Stacy DeBroff, best-selling author of *The Mom Book*, *The Mom Book Goes to School*, and *Mom Central: The Ultimate Family Organizer*, CEO and founder of Mom Central

NO REGRETS PARENTING

No Regrets Parenting

Turning Long Days and Short Years into Cherished Moments with Your Kids

Harley A. Rotbart, MD

Andrews McMeel
PUBLISHING®
www.andrewsmcmeel.com

Andrews McMeel Publishing
a division of Andrews McMeel Universal
1130 Walnut Street, Kansas City, Missouri 64106

www.andrewsmcmeel.com

Dr. Rotbart invites you to send your own comments and suggestions for *No Regrets Parenting* to his interactive blog at www.NoRegretsParenting.com.

ISBN: 978-1-4494-8917-5

Book design by Diane Marsh
Illustration by Sarah Coleman

ATTENTION: SCHOOLS AND BUSINESSES
Andrews McMeel books are available at quantity discounts with bulk purchase for educational, business, or sales promotional use. For information, please e-mail the Andrews McMeel Publishing Special Sales Department: specialsales@amuniversal.com.

DEDICATION

To my wife, Sara, for making the special moments
with our kids even more special.

To our parents, Helen, Max, Ruth, and Gene, for showing us how;
and to our kids, Matt, Emily, and Sam, for showing us why.

From generation to generation.

"LIFE IS A SUM OF ALL YOUR CHOICES."

—Albert Camus
French author and philosopher
1913–1960

"WE'VE HAD BAD LUCK WITH OUR KIDS. THEY'VE ALL GROWN UP."

—Christopher Morley
American novelist and poet
1890–1957

Contents

Acknowledgments

My deep gratitude goes to the parents and kids I've had the good fortune to work with as a pediatrician over the past thirty years; they have provided me with a front-row seat from which to observe best parenting practices. And to my colleagues—devoted pediatricians, family practitioners, psychologists, social workers, and nurses—my sincere appreciation for your role modeling and inspiration. Thanks to Diane Debrovner at *Parents* magazine for opening doors for me; to Lisa Leshne at The Leshne Agency for adopting me and talking me down from my bursts of author angst; and to Chris Schillig and the editorial board at Andrews McMeel for finding relevance in my writing. To the rest of the Andrews McMeel Publishing team, thank you for your skill and professionalism. I am grateful for the support of family and friends, especially Dean, Talya, Maxwell, Avital, Bill, Laurie, Carolyn, Becky, Joanie, Ron, Bernd, Donald, Barbara, Samantha, Dick, Linda, and Lizzy (who slept on her rug as I wrote). Finally, thanks and much love to Nurit for bringing a wonderful new dimension to our parenting.

Introduction—
Long Days, Short Years

The ten o'clock news hasn't even started, but you're too exhausted to watch; who can stay awake that late?! Car pools, lunch bags, after-school activities, dinner, homework, bath time, bedtime. All on top of your own job (or jobs!) and the other realities of adulthood. You have just enough energy left to drag yourself to bed so you can wake early and start the grind all over again. Each day with young kids feels like a week, each week like a month.

But, as every new birthday passes, childhood seems to be streaking by at warp speed—five-month-olds become five-year-olds in the blink of an eye, and then fifteen-year-olds. The colorful mobiles hanging from their cribs morph into tricycles, which morph into driving permits.

And then, poof, they're gone.

Sunrise, sunset.

How can we possibly be working so hard to get through each crazy, chaotic day with our kids and yet have the years fly by so quickly? Everyone knows it, everyone bemoans it, yet no one seems to know how to slow down the years while cramming twenty-five hours into every day.

WHAT IS THIS BOOK?

I don't claim to know how to slow down time, either. But I do have some ideas about how to *maximize* and *optimize* the time you spend with your kids—while they are still tucked into their bedrooms where you can peek in on them each night before you go to sleep. This is not a book about protecting your adult priorities or nurturing your relationship with your spouse, per se. There are plenty of those books, and lots of advice out there about how to look out for *your* needs while still getting the kids to soccer practice on time. Rather, this is a book about how to prioritize your *kids'* needs within your adult schedules, and how to stretch and enhance the time you spend with your kids. And if you are able to manage those juggling acts, you'll discover something remarkable: You *will* be more successful in protecting adult time for yourself and your spouse, and you'll feel less guilty doing it. More important, you'll be able to look back and take pride in knowing that you squeezed every moment and memory out of your kids' childhoods and that your kids' memories of you are vivid and loving. *No Regrets Parenting*—you can't do it over again, at least with these same kids, so do it right the first time.

This is a how-to manual for time management with kids, from crib through college. It will help you navigate the mundane, exhausting routines of parenthood, and show you how to transform those routines into special parenting events. It's all about redefining "quality time," and that means understanding the important difference between *minutes* and *moments.*

WHO ARE *YOU*?

Before diving into *No Regrets Parenting*, you should answer one important question about yourself: Who are *you*?

I'm not asking who you want people to think you are, or who your parents want you to be. I'm not asking who you want to be when you grow up—as much as you may want to deny it, once you have your own kids, you are officially grown up.

Who are *you*? Answer honestly, because if you pretend to be someone you're not, you're going to catch up with yourself and be disappointed. To help you identify yourself, I've divided "you" into seven basic components, which I'm going to ask you to rank in order of importance. Here are some definitions to use in the upcoming ranking exercise: being a *breadwinner* means earning a living for yourself and your family; as a *child* yourself, you may see satisfying your parents' goals for you as an important priority and/or you may have increasing responsibilities for the care of your elderly parents; *friend*, for the purposes of this exercise, does not extend to your spouse or partner, who gets a separate category; your nonwork passion qualifies you as a *hobbyist*—in the garden, on the tennis court or hiking trail, scrapbooking, writing poetry, playing the piano, painting; being a *parent* or a *spouse (partner)* has obvious meaning; a *professional* is usually also a breadwinner, but many professionals see themselves and their work as more than simply earning a living.

Now, as a way of determining how you see yourself, rank these seven elements of *you*, with the highest priority on top, lowest priority on the bottom. I know many of you are all of these people at some time in your life, perhaps even at the same time in your life. But what is their *order of importance* to *you*?

- Breadwinner
- Child
- Friend
- Hobbyist
- Parent
- Professional
- Spouse (partner)

If in your most honest self-assessment you ranked *parent* as number one, or second only to *spouse (partner)*, you will find yourself at ease reading this book and you will embrace the ideas for turning scarce minutes into special moments with your kids. If, on the other hand, *parent* ranked lower than one or two on your list, *No Regrets Parenting* may initially make you feel a bit uneasy but, I hope, will motivate you to reconsider your priorities.

The intent of the advice in this book is to give you a practical and purposeful blueprint for squeezing every possible precious moment with your kids out of your hectic and harried life. If anything other than *spouse (partner)* topped *parent* on the list, you are not a bad person or even an atypical person—for many, parenting is important, but not most important. But if you have other priorities that are higher than your kids, some of my suggestions may at first ring hollow—and may even feel oppressive—because they ask you to rethink how you manage other aspects of your life. If, however, you remain open to new ideas, you will find important reasons and strategies in this book that will enable you to elevate the role that parenting plays in your life.

You may argue that being a professional first and/or making a good living as a breadwinner makes you a better parent. And that may well be true. But the goal of *No Regrets Parenting* is not just to make you a better parent. It's to make you a parent who is there with your kids from crib to college, without neglecting your other responsibilities. So someday when you look back at the times when your kids were little, you will have *No Regrets* about the choices you made. Nostalgia is normal and good; it means your kids' childhoods were loving and meaningful for you. But there should be *No Regrets*.

But what about your spouse or partner? Shouldn't he or she be the top priority in your life? How many sad stories have you heard of couples struggling in their relationship because their kids, careers, and other commitments are all-consuming? Yes, I hope your spouse or partner is also number one or two on your priority list. Any lower than that and you need a different resource to help work out those issues. *No Regrets Parenting* assumes that you and your partner are in synch in your relationship *and* in your goals to maximize the time you have with your kids. If you're on different pages in either of those areas, I hope reading this book together will help you harmonize your priorities and realize that being an intimate and integral part of your kids' lives will give you new opportunities to spend quality time with each other, as well. I would be thrilled to take credit for bringing you and your partner even closer together.

Know yourself, and stay true to yourself. This book is for those of you who shudder at the thought of your kids growing up too fast, leaving for college, becoming young adults. *No Regrets Parenting* arms you with the tools you need to meet those eventualities with contentment and fulfillment: contentment that comes with knowing you were there, with your kids, every moment that you could have been, and fulfillment that comes with knowing you created new, *cherished moments* that otherwise might have been lost in the quest for expediency. In fact, if you learn and apply the basics of *No Regrets Parenting*, you will greet your children's departure with a profound sense of satisfaction, knowing you have given them what they need to succeed, and given yourself what you need to feel like a successful parent. To be sure, you'll gaze into their empty bedrooms and miss them terribly when they leave home. But you won't have missed them when they were still *at* home.

The days are long, but the years are short. And now is the time.

HOW TO READ THIS BOOK

I may be unique as an author in suggesting that the bathroom can be an ideal spot to keep this little volume. The book is not written to be read cover to cover. In fact, what parent with young kids has the time, or the concentration, to read *anything* cover to cover? And since this book is all about time management and finding balance, each chapter is short and written to stand on its own. So, pick and choose, skip around. How much you read in a single sitting really depends on how long you need to be sitting . . . if you catch my meaning.

Alternatively, tuck the book into the glove box of your car and pull it out for a quick fix while you're in line at the drive-through or waiting in the school pickup zone. Or perch it on your nightstand for a little inspirational reading before sleep—although there is a clear risk that the book will get you so worked up about great new plans with your kids for tomorrow that you won't be able to fall asleep!

Part 1 of this book lays out the basic principles, and Part 2 provides specific strategies in the practice of *No Regrets Parenting*. Each part is important, but you should probably read the first part first. That's why it's the first part. Finally, Part 3, the Epilogue, launches you into the exciting world of parenting college kids.

STAY IN TOUCH

E-mail me with your own suggestions and brainstorms—I'll work as many of your ideas into my *No Regrets Parenting* blog as possible. Find my e-mail address, as well as the blog, at www. NoRegretsParenting.com.

No Regrets Parenting
Basic Principles

The Checkered History
of Parenting Advice

*L*ooking back at the evolution of parenting advice over the centuries, it seems to me that Adam and Eve may have been the only parents in history without the benefit of an "advice du jour" book on how to raise children. Admittedly, considering how things worked out for their kids, our original forebears probably could have used a book or two on the subject. But surely if Adam and Eve would have had *two* parenting books on their shelf in the garden, each book would have advocated a diametrically different parenting philosophy.

Seventeenth-century poet and nobleman John Walmot is famously quoted as saying, "Before I got married I had six theories about bringing up children; now I have six children and no theories." Parenting experts—from psychologists and pediatricians to philosophers, clergy, kings, queens, and First Ladies—have all opined in learned and not-so-learned treatises on how best to raise kids. Slow parenting, helicopter parenting, free-range parenting, and attachment parenting. Soccer moms, tiger moms, and stay-at-home dads. Nurturant parenting, strict parenting, ethical parenting, indulgent parenting, authoritative parenting, and authoritarian parenting. Spanking, praising, scolding, rewarding, tough love, and safety-net love. Another day, another dollar spent on another expert's theory.

So, what parenting philosophy should *you* use to raise *your* children? Forgive me, but I'm going to duck that question. Over the past thirty years as a pediatrician, when it seemed appropriate, I have given parenting advice to young parents (and not-so-young parents), using my doctor's intuition to judge the individual circumstances and choose the best parenting approach to suggest. At home with our own three kids, my wife and I have relied on our parenting intuition, probably crisscrossing through a hodgepodge of experts' recommendations without even knowing it. And in the end, I have concluded that there is no single "right" way to raise kids. The unique circumstances and dynamics in your household will guide you in developing your own parenting intuition, or they may even guide you toward a book from a particular parenting guru whose advice best fits your family. There is, however, a single truth that applies to any parenting philosophy you may choose: *Your kids need you to be there.* They need to see who you are and how you live your life. And in return, they will help you to *better* see who you are and how you *should* live your life.

So, now for a question that I won't duck: How can you be there for your kids in the way they need you and in the way you need them? The simple answer: Find enough time. Regardless of the approach to parenting you choose, the moments you have with your kids are fleeting and precious. This book doesn't deal much with particular parenting philosophies. This is a book about *time*—finding enough of it and making the most of it.

Precious Moments and the "Other" Biological Clock

*W*hen you add up all the time your kids spend at day care, in school, asleep, at friends' homes, with babysitters, at camp, and otherwise occupied with activities that don't include you, the remaining moments in their days become especially precious. There are only 940 Saturdays between a child's birth and her leaving for college. Though that may sound like a lot, how many have you already used up? If your child is five years old, 260 Saturdays are gone. Poof! How did you spend them? And the older your kids get, the busier their Saturdays get with friends and activities. Ditto Sundays.

And what about weekdays? Are you kidding?! Depending on your child's age, there may be as few as one or two hours a day during the week for you to spend with him. When kids are very young, they sleep through many of your hours together. When they're a little older, school, homework, your work schedule, and their playdates turn Mondays into Fridays with little time to catch your breath, or catch up with your kids.

This inexorable march of time that turns babies into big kids, and big kids into young adults, is the "other" biological clock facing young couples. Once the miracle of childbirth occurs, every day brings new growth, new milestones, and new wonderment. But the challenges of juggling our adult lives often prevent us from fully appreciating the delicate nuances of childhood. Yet the biological clock of parenthood continues to tick.

How are you spending the time you have with your young kids? Are they watching TV while you're doing the laundry or preparing dinner? Are they playing computer games while you're catching up on e-mail? Do you take them in the car on your errands with a DVD performing hypnosis in the backseat? Do you resent the distractions from your daily routine that the kids cause? If you answered yes to any of those questions, it's time to readjust your inner clock: Stop counting "minutes spent" with your kids and start accumulating "moments shared." Don't measure the time you allow yourself to spend with your kids each day, but rather how you made that time memorable. The strategies in Part 2 of this book will help you take scarce minutes and turn them into special moments—cherished moments that, in the aggregate, will leave you fulfilled and satisfied when the kids are grown.

Here's a mental trick to help you readjust your thinking from *minutes* to *moments*. In the course of each bedtime's bedlam, try to see into the future. The next time the clamor crescendos, but before the din dims, imagine your biological parenthood clock wound forward to the time when they're grown and have left home. Picture their formerly tousled bedrooms as neat, clean, and empty. See the tidy backseat of the car, vacuumed and without crumbs or Cheerios. Playroom shelves neatly stacked with dusty toys. Laundry under control. Then wind the imaginary clock back from the future to now, and see these minutes of mayhem for what they are, finite and fleeting moments. Never to be reproduced. Precious.

3D Parenting

There are days when it seems that all you do is get frustrated with your kids and fail to find your parental equilibrium. Of course, you know what you're supposed to do. You're supposed to be a role model of reason and patience. Wise and understanding, yet firm and principled. And then they'll throw a temper tantrum when you're already late for work, fight with their siblings for the "best" seat at the dinner table, beg for candy in the supermarket line, and refuse—absolutely refuse—to change their clothes, brush their hair, or eat their dinner.

Those are the times when parents often resort to 3D parenting: distraction, distortion, and deception. Yes, sometimes these may be necessary evils, the price of doing the business of parenthood. You really need your kids to do something NOW!, go somewhere FAST!, or just LEAVE YOU ALONE! for a few minutes. So you exaggerate the urgency, hyperbolize their intransigence, say mean things you don't mean, make deals and promises you know you'll never keep, or put them in front of the TV rather than hear one more whiny protest. I know, I've been there many times. This is not a holier-than-thou sermon, I promise.

Here's the problem with those 3Ds: Your kids lose their trust in you. Not all at once, and not if you slip into the Ds only once in awhile, dealing with your kids honestly and without sleight of hand most of the time. But gradually, the more you resort to distraction, distortion, and deception, the less strong the bond of trust between you and your kids will be. They are more likely to distract, distort, and deceive in their relationship with you as they grow older.

There's a solution to this problem. Replace those dark Ds with a set of three good and healthy Ds: defer, decompress, and deliver. At the height of tension and frustration, when you've simply got to be somewhere or get something accomplished, and when you feel your inner barometer rising, don't deal with the deeper issues. *Defer* them to later that day, *decompress* the immediate crisis, and then *deliver* on your promise to resolve the issue under calmer circumstances. Your kids will get the message that you respect them, take their feelings seriously, and can be taken at your word. No trickery just to get through the crisis—rather an honest commitment to fix the problem together. Later.

By the time later comes around, make sure you don't forget your pledge. Although by then, because kids really do live in the moment, they may have completely forgotten the earlier crisis du jour. Call your child into a quiet spot, sit next to each other, and offer to discuss whatever was upsetting her and whatever was upsetting you. How much better is this quality time together, calmly discussing the issue, than the time you would have wasted earlier in the day had you continued the fight? When you realize how short the time we have with our kids really is, how many of those precious minutes, days, and weekends do you want lost to battles of wills and wars of words?

If she is still bothered when you meet later that day, work to fix it with her. If she has moved on, tell her you love her, tell her how you expect her to handle the next upset (remember, you are the parent and it's your job to teach correct behavior). And then move on with her.

Guilt and Worries

*P*arenting is among the greatest sources of human joy; it is also the single greatest cause of guilt and worry. Not only do we feel guilty about the things we've done or not done for our kids from the time they were born, but we also feel guilty about the genes we've burdened our kids with *before* they were born. And we worry about everything we can and can't control in our kids' lives. So there it is. Whatever our kids become or fail to become, achieve or fail to achieve is our responsibility. Their health and happiness, sense of self, respect for others, and the course they chart for their lives all rest on our shoulders. Or so it seems. Whenever she would see a newborn, my grandmother would ask rhetorically, in her gentle European accent, "From this they have to make a person?"

It's impossible to fully alleviate you of your sense of guilt. Beginning with your baby's first diaper rash, you'll assume it's your fault for not changing her frequently enough. And it's downhill from there. And then there's the worry. Will they be happy and healthy and make wise choices? Will fate smile fondly on them? Will they associate with the right people? Have you taught them how to handle all the difficult and dangerous situations that will come up in their lives?

Here's the good news: By practicing *No Regrets Parenting*, you are hereby completely absolved of one form of guilt. No, not for the diaper rash. You are absolved of any guilt you might feel about not spending enough time with your kids. *No Regrets Parenting* is about opportunities, many realized, but some missed. If you find the minutes to do even a fraction of the suggestions in this book, you will have captured precious moments that would otherwise have been lost. And if you do more than a fraction of the suggestions? When the long days with your young kids are over, the years will not have seemed quite so short.

This is very important, so please read it carefully: You should never feel guilty about the minutes you can't spare, the times when you are too busy, and the moments that are lost to the realities of life despite your best efforts. *No Regrets Parenting* doesn't ask you to be superhuman; it only asks that you set the right priorities for your time and make the conscious effort to be there as often as possible for your kids. To help you with that, try the ideas in Part 2 of this book. Some may work for your family, others won't. Along the way you'll invent your own strategies for turning scarce minutes into cherished moments. The only guilt you should ever feel is from not trying.

And here's another reason not to feel guilty. Kids need to grow their independence. Whenever you start to feel badly about leaving them with the babysitter, or dropping them at a friend's house where the friend's parent supervises the playdate, or putting them in front of the TV while you pull the house together, STOP THE GUILT TRIP! You're not neglecting them or failing as a *No Regrets* parent because you're not with them 24/7. Rather, you're providing balance between the time they spend *with* you and the time they need *away* from you to develop independence. And kids need to know they don't have a claim on all of your time—the goal of *No Regrets Parenting* is appreciative kids and fulfilled parents, not entitled kids and guilt-ridden parents.

What about the worries? So much of parents' worries are rooted in whether their kids are adequately prepared for the challenges they will face in their lives. *No Regrets Parenting* should ease some of those worries, too. The more time you spend with your kids, the more they see how you confront and overcome challenges; and, the better they understand from you how to set priorities in their own lives, the less you have to worry about. Be the kind of person you hope your kids will become. And then spend enough time with them that they learn how to become that person.

There are three kinds of worries in the world: kid worries, grown-up worries, and worries that are completely out of anyone's hands (the weather, for example). Kids should worry only about kid worries and leave the grown-up worries to their parents. Parents should worry only about those things that are within their control. *No Regrets Parenting* gives you more control over many of the worries you have for your kids. With your love, your time, and your role modeling for them, you can sleep better knowing you have given them the foundation they need for the challenges that will come.

And as for those worries over which we truly have no control? It won't help to worry about them, so don't.

Your Legacy

What will your kids remember about their childhoods—and about your role in them? My wife's grandmother was famous for periodically telling her daughters, "Remember, girls, you're having a happy childhood." What will your legacy be when your kids tell *their* kids about you?

Leave your kids with warm, glowing, and loving memories of the times they spent with you. When they leave for college or their other adult pursuits, they should be able to look back and recall the intimacy and depth, the laughter and lessons, the traditions and values of their relationships with you. They should feel so connected to you that they strive to use the same formulas and strategies that you used with them to create permanent and indelible bonds with their own kids. How thrilling it will be for you as a grandparent someday to hear your own words coming from your child, now speaking to her own kids! Of course, your kids will do an even better job with their kids than you did with yours—isn't that the point?

Most important, your legacy depends on your kids really knowing you. That can happen only if they spend enough meaningful time with you to hear what you think, see what you do, and learn what you have to teach.

The Villagers

This may sound a little old-fashioned, but I believe that kids who get 100 percent from their parents turn out, on average, to be better adjusted, happier, and more satisfied adults. And the parents of those kids have the blessing of knowing that their kids' successes are not coincidences. A former First Lady famously titled her book *It Takes a Village,** paraphrasing an African proverb about the many cooperative efforts required to raise children. Indeed, the community your kids experience can provide them with an important sense of belonging and stability. But, again, I plead guilty to old-fashionism. Even though many villagers may participate in your kids' formative years, you are their most important guidepost, mentor, and friend. Relying too heavily on others for those roles is risky and, ultimately, unfulfilling.

Your kids' village is diverse, unfocused, and conflicted in its priorities. First of all, every village has its idiots who may negatively impact your kids, either intentionally or unintentionally; you have to be there to undo their influences. Of course, as Hillary Rodham Clinton wrote, there are many villagers who can positively impact your kids—day-care providers, playgroup parents, teachers, classmates, clergy, coaches, college counselors, etc. They each have their own well-meaning agendas for your kids. But you must be the filter, finding the

---

* Hillary Rodham Clinton, *It Takes a Village: And Other Lessons Children Teach Us* (New York: Simon & Schuster, 1996).

right balance of influences so your kids get the right messages. The villagers also have worries and distractions to deal with in their own lives. None are committed to your kids wholly and solely. That's your job alone, and your privilege.

What Do Your Kids Need from You?

This is your pediatrician speaking. In the nearly three decades I have been working with parents and children, the two most frequently asked questions have been:

1. What do my kids need most from me?

2. What must I do to be a good parent?

The answer to the first question is simple, and the answer to the second is simpler still. Years of research in child development and growth have identified *eight essential requirements* for kids to become happy, successful adults. For all the research and all the scholarly writings, there are no surprises here—you already intuitively know these fundamentals of parenting. Your kids need:

SECURITY—Kids must feel safe and sound. This means providing them with basic survival needs: shelter, food, clothing, medical care, and protection from harm.

CONSISTENCY—Parents must synchronize their parenting. No "good cop, bad cop." Deliver a singular message to your kids as their parents, not separately as their mom and dad. Consistency also means that important values are important values, and should not be changed casually or for convenience.

STABILITY—Ideally, a family remains together in a stable household throughout kids' childhoods. But even when that ideal breaks down, your child's life must be as little disrupted as possible. Stability also comes from community. Kids and families should be part of larger units to give them a sense of belonging and cultural continuity.

EMOTIONAL SUPPORT—Parents' words and deeds must engender in their kids trust, respect, self-esteem, and, ultimately, independence. In many families, parents also provide spiritual guidance in accordance with their own beliefs and values.

LOVE—Specialists rightly say that unwavering demonstration and expression of love for your kids can overcome almost any parenting "mistakes" you might make. Even when your kids have disobeyed, angered, frustrated, and rebelled against you, they must know that you love them and that you will always love them.

EDUCATION—It is your obligation and your challenge to make sure your kids get the best possible education to ensure their futures. This, of course, includes school. But it also includes the invaluable lessons about life that you can provide during the time you spend together. They learn by what they hear you say and by what they see you do.

POSITIVE ROLE MODELS—It's hard to say enough about the importance of role modeling. As parents, you are your kids' first and most important role models. In addition to everything they learn from you about being good kids and good people, they are also watching how you parent. An undercurrent of this book is that if you find a way to make the most of every precious moment you have with your kids, not only will you raise wonderful kids, but you also will be showing them how to be wonderful parents themselves someday. Kids parent the way they were parented. Show them how important your time with them is, and you will impact generations to come.

STRUCTURE—Rules, boundaries, and limits. Without them, kids are forced to be adults before they are ready, and they lose respect for you and other adults.

So, those are the eight essential requirements of kids. Now for the second question: What do you need to do to be a good parent? Easy—provide for your kids' eight essential requirements! How? With *time*, the miracle solution for most dilemmas of childhood and parenthood—and the basis for this book. Time spent with your kids, taken in fleeting minutes or leisurely hours, gives you the opportunity to provide your kids with security, stability, consistency, emotional support, love, education, role modeling, and structure. The converse is also true—not spending enough or the right kind of time with your kids deprives them of some or all of their basic needs. Equally important, not spending enough or the right kind of time with your kids deprives *you* of the wonderful privileges of parenting.

Part 2 of this book is all about finding that time.

Your Report Card

There are no grades given for parenting. No honor roll announced, no certificates awarded, no degrees granted. You don't have to prove your parenting prowess to anyone except yourself. Sure, your toddler may throw a fit or two in protest of your rules. Your teenagers will very likely weigh in, sometimes quite demonstrably, on your parenting skills. And your adult kids will inevitably reflect on their childhoods and on your parenting. But ultimately it's your opinion about your parenting that matters most, because you're the one who will walk past their empty rooms when they're grown, and you're the one who will reminisce over their baby pictures on the wall. Not every day with your kids will be perfect; in fact, many days with your kids won't be perfect. As we say in our house, some days you eat the bear, and other days the bear eats you. But your report card isn't a daily reckoning—it's a cumulative performance evaluation. And this is one of those rare situations in life in which you grade your own final exam.

When you have the time and energy to look back, how will you feel about yourself, your parenting, and the years you had with your kids? How will your self–report card turn out? Will you lament the time wasted, the opportunities missed, and the special moments that passed you by? Or will you have peace of mind, knowing that you did everything in your power to be there with your kids, to be the best parent possible, to give your kids every ounce of you that you were able to share?

This is neither a blame game nor a guilt trip. Truth be told, your kids don't need you constantly around to develop into decent, accomplished, and grateful adults. And there are certainly circumstances in which parents' best intentions and efforts don't turn out as hoped. Circumstances in which nature trumps nurture, or in which twists and turns of life that are out of your control take your kids in the wrong direction. But even then, if you have made the most of your time with your kids and given everything you have to give, you'll never have to ask, "Was there more I should have done?"

When you take the red pencil to grade your final exam, make sure you'll be able to write in bold letters across the top: *No Regrets.*

"Quality" vs. "Quantity" Time

*B*eginning famously with the Baby Boomers and continuing with Generation X and Generation Y, parents have compensated for having so little *quantity* of time to spend with their children by invoking "quality time." Quality time usually means brief and choreographed bursts of activity dedicated intensively and exclusively to the kids—and when those bursts expire, the kids get dropped off in front of the TV or at the babysitter's. Two hours at the nature preserve. An afternoon at the theater. Dinner at a fancy restaurant. Today's "quality time" is often pricey because parents' expectations for those minutes with their kids are so high. Black and white: It's time with the kids, or it's time without the kids. This book, though, will show you the grays, and redefine "quality time" for busy, working parents. Time at work needn't be devoid of kid time, and time at home may involve work, but both settings can include your kids in ways that benefit everyone, and both can help define a *new* "quality time."

Professional lives spent moving up the ladder of success, or even treading water to maintain financial stability, have left little time for coddling and cuddling. Two-career family situations are especially hard on the quantity of time available for home life, making the "quality" option of short, structured spurts of time with the kids seem like the only alternative. Adult responsibilities are realities. I will not advise you to handcuff your professional life or sacrifice your financial security "for the sake of the kids"—although you may choose to make some of those compromises because your priorities guide you in that direction. But you don't have to give up being a successful grown-up to be a successful parent. Rather, Part 2 of this book will show you how to make the most of every minute that you do spend with your kids, and how to include the kids in more of your minutes than you may have thought possible. Quality time needn't be expensive; in fact, as you'll read in the upcoming chapter "Money," the best experiences with your kids are usually free.

All the strategies for the *new* "quality time" that follow in Part 2 of this book need to be put into an age-appropriate context, in which common sense rules. Most of the suggestions can be adapted and modified to fit the ages of your kids—kitchen duty, for example. At the youngest ages, sharing quality kitchen time with your kids may mean your infant finger feeding himself Cheerios in the high chair while you cook; but helping you cook will come with growth. Texting with your kids is obviously designed for when they're a little older, but other digital interactions can begin even at the youngest ages when your kids can sit on your lap as you work your laptop. The actual activity you and your kids share together is much less important than the togetherness that you share in all of these activities.

So, let's agree that from this page forward, the *new* "quality time" means meaningful and memorable time, regardless of duration or content. Quality time may occur when you least expect it—yes, at the nature preserve, but also in the minivan on the way to ballet practice, and during commercials of your favorite family TV show. Although you may use your newfound quality time for teaching your kids life lessons, addressing their crises, or planning the upcoming weekend, most of the quality time you discover in this book is unscripted and spontaneous. By the time the kids are in college, quality time may have to be phone time. Even then, unscripted and spontaneous is important. When our oldest left for college, there were so many things we needed to hear about when he called, and so much advice and encouragement we felt we needed to give him, we forgot about unscripted and spontaneous time. Until he reminded us—"Guys, can we just talk about baseball for a few minutes? How 'bout that Colorado Rockies shortstop?!"

The purpose of Part 2 of this book is to guide you in creating ample opportunities for *new* "quality time" with your kids, despite your hectic lives and chaotic schedules. And when you accomplish that goal, your kids' next birthdays won't seem to have passed as quickly.

Independence and
Subliminal Togetherness

The more time you spend with your kids, taking advantage of every precious moment, the less time they are on their own, learning lessons of independence. Kids need plenty of time alone and with friends to explore their environment and to establish their identities. Yet, they also need lots of time with you to learn *how* to explore and establish. They learn by watching you, listening to you, and imitating you. This presents a real conundrum for parents wanting to slow down the years without slowing down their child's maturation.

So . . . how can you achieve a healthy balance with your kids between independence and togetherness? How can you avoid "helicopter" parenting, hovering around them all the time, while still enjoying as much time together as you can squeeze in before they're off on their own?

The "Calendars" section in Part 2 of this book guides you in using your kids' schedules to help set your own—prioritizing their events and their schedules, and trying to work your commitments around theirs so you can be there for the important adventures in their lives. But, although your goal should be to never miss their big karate matches or class plays, you *should* miss those times in your kids' lives when they need space to grow and learn independently. School, of course, gives them plenty of time away from you—but those hours are highly programmed and less amenable to independent exploration.

Give your young kids downtime with toys or TV when they come home from school, and plenty of playdates with friends during which you, or their friends' parents, are in another room keeping an eye and ear on them from a distance. Let them play and explore in the fenced backyard where you can see them through the windows, and at the playground with you watching from the nearby park bench. Youth sports programs help your kids develop independence and social skills. At the right age, and with appropriate safeguards, wandering on the Internet and Facebook is a very "today" version of independence. When they're adolescents, the closed door to their rooms should be respected—privacy for teens must be indulged and endured by parents, within limits, of course. Separation times like these also give you "sanity breaks."

But the best of all worlds are those situations in which your kids can be independent, with you at their sides or in their shadows. Let's call this shared-but-separate state of being *subliminal togetherness.* The idea is that you and your kids are sharing new and interesting experiences without your kids feeling your presence or being subjected to your real-time interpretations and lessons. They form their impressions and learn from their environment, without your influence. Or at least without your influence being obvious. Your kids' first rafting trip is a similar experience for them whether you are also on the raft or they go with friends. You get to see your kids' first trip down the river and can talk about it with them on the car ride home, but the excitement and energy they feel is all their own. Or their first lemonade stand, with you supervising from the living room window, available for consultation and replenishment of ice as needed. "Hire" your child as "mom's helper," letting him look after younger siblings or neighbors' kids while you're elsewhere in the house taking care of your chores and listening in as your child grows into his new responsibilities; this is a great time to dust off the baby monitor you used when they were in their cribs and playpens. Train the new puppy with your kids—

they'll be so excited about teaching their pet that they won't notice that you are teaching them *how* to teach; and then take the dog for walks together. Help coach your children's sports team or be the scoutmaster for their Brownies or Cub Scout troops, participating side by side with them without restricting the growth and maturation they get from being part of a team. When your kids are old enough to have driving permits, drive with them as often as you can. They will be so excited and terrified to finally be driving a car that they'll barely notice you—that is, until you scream that they just ran a red light! Subliminal togetherness.

As your kids get older, their truly independent time will quickly increase, and your together time with them will just as quickly decrease. They'll go on the raft trips without you, exchange their lemonade stand for real summer jobs, grow from "mom's helpers" to full-fledged babysitters, and replace their learner's permits with real driver's licenses. All of that is as it should be, and all the more reason to make the most of your time together at all ages of their childhood.

Best Friend or Parent?

Are you your kids' best friend or are you their parent? Many have written about the risks of being your children's best friend—overindulgence, underdiscipline, failure to set limits or establish structure in your kids' lives. Those admonitions are true. We can never lose sight of our parenting responsibilities, even when those put us into the bad-guy role, which they frequently do.

But this is another one of those situations in which it's not either/or —we should always be our kids' best friends, too. Each parent is *both* good cop and bad cop—those roles should never be divided up between two parents. Never be afraid to scold if doing so teaches and protects your kids. Don't shy away from disciplining kids—they have to, and want to, respect you even if they "hate" you for a few minutes for telling them no. But as necessary as the bad cop is, the good cop is even more important for you and for your kids. By being there during their big moments and little moments alike, making sure they have plenty of belly laughs and giggles, and being available to patiently advise and teach, we show our kids they can trust us not just as parents, but as friends. Best friends.

The more we know about our kids' lives, the more valuable we become when they have worries or crises. We know their friends' names and which kids are the school bullies; we know the quirks of our kids' teachers, the lunchroom menu, and the schedule for student council elections. Soon enough, friends their own age will become your kids' confidants and consultants—but when that transition occurs, the close relationships you have built with your kids will bring them back to you for the big issues and even for some of the smaller ones. When your kids feel you are actively engaged in their lives, because you have had ample time with them to truly listen and absorb, they will feel comfortable entering into each new discussion with you—they won't feel that "you just don't get it, Mom," because you do get it. You know the players and the play, so each new scene starts in a familiar setting.

That's what being a best friend is all about.

Designer Children—Nature vs. Nurture

*Y*ou want your kids to be smart, talented, kind, responsible, well mannered, loving, athletic, humble, generous, funny, and good-looking, right? Not a problem. There are hundreds of books and Web sites out there to help with each of those child designs and more. *Raising a Studious Child, Creating Nicer Kids, Teaching Your Children to Love, Growing Your Child's Natural Talents, The Well-Groomed Child Within, Taming the Stubborn Child, Liberating the Shy Child,* etc. Of course, I made up those titles, and any resemblance to actual child-design books is purely accidental. But you get the point. Many gurus will tell you how to mold, fix, and tailor your kids into the perfect little angels, or robots, you are hoping for. I'm not smart enough to be able to do that, so I have a much simpler, two-step approach:

FIRST STEP—Embrace nature. Teach your kids to accept and be grateful for the gifts nature gave them. Every child is born with a genetic "package," over which he or she has no choice. One of our most poignant moments with our daughter was a teary one, sitting with her on the edge of her bed, six years old, discussing "packages." Sure, sweetheart, there might be things you would change about yourself if you could. There are the things Mommy and Daddy were born with that they like a lot, and there are the things Mommy and Daddy got in their "packages" that they don't like as much—or even hate, sometimes. And your best friend whom you really wish you could look more like? When you look at her *whole* "package," are you sure you really want to be her? Look at all the wonderful things you got in your "package" that you would never, ever change. Aren't you glad you're you?

SECOND STEP—Provide nurture. Be the type of person you want your children to become, and then spend plenty of time with them so they can learn from your role modeling. After your kids are born, tiny "packages" of natural gifts, the world around them takes over, nurturing and determining the kind of people they will be. Parents are the most important nurturers in their kids' worlds, and the most influential in shaping their future selves. Children are sponges, soaking up conscious and unconscious lessons that you teach them.

Design your children well, by your example.

Brain Buttons

I am a physician, but what I'm about to tell you is not based on anatomy or neurobiology or medicine. It's based on my experience as a parent and my observations of the kids and parents I've cared for over the past thirty years. Kids' brains are too cluttered, chaotic, cloudy, and complicated to properly register most of what you are trying to communicate to them most of the time. Your kids' eyes may be open, but often there's nobody home. While you're hoping they are absorbing the pearls of wisdom you're dispensing, they are zoned out in a parallel universe where they keep doing the same stupid things despite your repeated teaching, preaching, and beseeching. Teaching, preaching, and beseeching are important, to be sure. But for effective *No Regrets Parenting*, there is a secret for permanently imprinting your kids' brains with the lessons you are teaching them, and with wonderful feelings and memories of their time with you. How is that possible if your kids are in perpetual brain freeze?

The best way to cut through the fog in their brains and reach your kids' centers of understanding and appreciation is by pushing their three hidden attention buttons. First, the "fun button." Kids start to pay attention, and therefore are better able to learn and remember, when they are enjoying themselves. It's as if their brains don't want to miss any of the fun, so they lock in on whatever is going on while they're having fun. Enjoying themselves is what kids do for a living, so this strategy for getting through to them is easy. If you want them to learn about safely crossing the street, teach them while crossing the street on the way to the ice cream store or the amusement park. Not only will they learn to look both ways, but they'll also remember that you made learning fun and yummy. What a great parent you are! More important, you remember how much fun being a parent can be, and how vital what you have to teach your kids is for their safety and for their futures.

Don't forget to laugh with your kids—boisterous, booming belly laughs. Laughter bonds like no other activity in life. Laughter boosts your immune system (trust me, I'm a doctor) and extends your life (trust me, same reason). Laughter pushes your kids' "fun buttons," helping them focus and listen to you. Be goofy, play practical jokes, tickle, watch slapstick movies. Learn magic tricks to amaze your kids and their friends; turn the sprinkler on them; dress up in funny clothes or silly hats to surprise them. There's nothing like hearing your kids tell their friends, "This is my dad—he's funny!" And while they (and you) are having fun, they are more receptive than ever to what you are trying to teach them.

Another underappreciated attention switch in your kids' brains is their "audit button." It's flipped on whenever they watch you in your daily activities: working, driving, cooking, cleaning, playing, relaxing, speaking, and showing your love. If you don't think your kids are scrutinizing what you do, try uttering a curse word or throwing a dish in a fit of anger. Your behavior will be mimicked and your poorly chosen words parroted. Politeness, affection, pride, confidence, patience, tolerance, morality, respect, and self-control will also be mimicked. Our youngest child's first complex sentence came when he was sitting in his car seat running errands with Mom. He was holding a toy plastic phone, put it to his ear, and said, "Driving car pool, be little late." When people say how much your kids remind them of you, make sure that's a compliment.

You turn on the "mosey button" in your kids' brains when you s . . . l . . . o . . . w   d . . . o . . . w . . . n. We overload our kids, and ourselves, with the deadlines and dance card of each day. Kids can't lock in or focus when they're rushing. Set aside daily moseying time. Mosey through dinner, mosey for an evening walk after dinner, mosey during story time. The extra few minutes you devote to eating slower, walking slower, and reading slower will give your kids' brains a breather and let them better appreciate their time with you, and vice versa. It's true that just being able to gather everyone at the same table for dinner is a difficult feat, and after-dinner commitments feel pressing. But chew a little slower and linger a little longer—even fifteen extra minutes can make the difference between a "functional" dinner and an enjoyable family event. Stretch the bedtime story a few minutes longer, too. If you're looking at your watch while you're reading to your kids, they'll sense the rush and you will lose the magic of the moment.

It's especially important to mosey during listening time, whenever that occurs in your kids' day; so important that there's a whole chapter coming up called "Listening." As hard as it may be sometimes, try not to rush your kids when they're telling you about their days, their accomplishments, or their worries. Give them your undivided attention—you won't have to do it for long because they'll tire of talking and move on to their next activities. But while they are in a sharing mood, share.

Traditions

ussian scientist Ivan Pavlov became famous at the turn of the twentieth century for discovering and characterizing what he called the "conditioned reflex." Simply put, if dogs became accustomed to hearing a bell ring immediately before he fed them, soon the dogs began to anticipate their meals, salivating at the sound of the bell before ever seeing or smelling the food. That's the way traditions begin; those dogs probably told their puppies to listen carefully for ringing bells because of the wonderful things that happen when that occurs.

Traditions are conditioned reflexes. Throughout Part 2 of this book, you will find suggestions for establishing family traditions that will trigger happy anticipation and leave lasting, cherished memories. Traditions around major holidays and minor holidays. Bedtime, bathtime, and mealtime traditions; sports and pastime traditions; birthday and anniversary traditions; charitable and educational traditions.

If your family's traditions coincide with others' observances, such as celebrating Thanksgiving, you will still make those traditions unique to your family because of the personal nuances you add. Volunteering at the food bank on Thanksgiving morning, measuring and marking their heights on the door frame in the basement, Grandpa's artistic carving of the turkey, and their uncle's famous gravy are the traditions our kids salivated about when they were younger, and still do on their long plane rides home at the end of November each year. (By the way, our dog Lizzy has confirmed Pavlov's observations; when the carving knife turns on, cue the saliva, tail wagging, and doggy squealing.)

But don't limit your family's traditions to the big and obvious events like Thanksgiving. Weekly taco nights, family book club and movie nights, pajama walks, ice cream sundaes on Sundays, backyard football during halftime of TV games, pancakes in Mom and Dad's bed on weekends, leaf fights in the fall, walks to the sledding hill on the season's first snow, Chinese food on anniversaries, Indian food for big occasions, and balloons hanging from the ceiling around the breakfast table on birthday mornings. Be creative, even silly. Make a secret family noise together when you're the only ones in the elevator. When you share a secret that "can't leave this room," everybody knows to reach up in the air and grab the imaginary tidbit before it can get away. Have a family comedy night or a talent show on each birthday. Make holiday cards from scratch. Celebrate major family events by writing personalized lyrics to an old song and karaoking your new composition together.

There are two keys to establishing family traditions: repetition and anticipation. When you find something that brings out excitement and smiles in your kids, keep doing it. Not so often that it becomes mundane, but on a regular and predictable enough basis that it becomes an ingrained part of the family repertoire. And begin talking about the traditional event days ahead of time so by the time it finally happens, your kids are beside themselves with excitement. Anticipation can be as much fun as the tradition itself.

The Parenting Meditation

*B*y now you have realized that turning scarce minutes into cherished moments and redefining quality time are our goals. You're trying hard to be there for big events and small events, creating enduring traditions and lifelong memories. But here's a disturbing truth: Even if you attempt the impossible—doing *everything* I recommend in Part 2 of this book—it won't be enough. Unless you are really paying attention. Paying attention to your kids' childhoods, and to your parenthood, will be the toughest assignment I give you.

As Far Eastern customs and culture have found their way to those of us in Western countries, meditation and mindfulness may have become familiar concepts to you. But even if you've heard the terminology, and even if you've tried the practice, you probably have never considered applying them to parenting. But *No Regrets Parenting* requires its own special form of mindfulness and meditation.

Here's the reason: I hope that, perhaps with the help of this book, you will quickly learn to navigate family life and schedules well enough to salvage substantial time with your kids that otherwise would be lost in the everyday mayhem and madness. That's the good news. The bad news is that you may be so overwhelmed with the responsibilities and complexities of parenthood that you toggle into automatic pilot, oblivious to the wonders you have created. If your mind is elsewhere during the precious moments that you have worked so hard to preserve, you have lost your kids' childhoods just as sure as if you hadn't spent the time with them at all.

And it's easy for that to happen. With your kids in the kitchen helping you make dinner, your mind is taking you back to this morning at the office, or pushing you ahead to tomorrow's busy agenda. By the time you realize that you've zoned out, dinner is finished and the kids are upstairs doing homework. What did they say to you? What did you answer? What are they worried about? Did you comfort them? Your walk in the park with them on a weekend morning is serene and soothing—unless you're still obsessing about the fight you had with your spouse, or about preparing your taxes, or paying your utility bill. When you get back, your kids dash off to play with friends and you're not sure if you held hands with them on your walk, if you stopped at the playground, or even if you remembered to ask them about the bully who's been bothering them at school. You rush from work to get to their soccer game but don't notice them playing because you're thinking about what you didn't finish before you left. You film their birthday parties but don't even see what the video camera sees because you're thinking you should be cutting the lawn or fixing the car.

Sure, you can pat yourself on the back for involving the kids in dinnertime preparation, walking with them in the park, getting to their soccer practice, and being there for their birthdays—but why bother? You missed those events even though you were there!

The traditional practice of mindful meditation teaches how to clear your head of the torrents of distracting thoughts that constantly interject themselves, or at least to acknowledge the distractions and dismiss them. It's not easy. The most common approach is to focus on the involuntary act of breathing. By paying attention to something that usually requires no attention at all, despite occurring ten to twenty times every minute, the brain is given a focal point from which extraneous thoughts can be excluded. The goal is, in meditation jargon, "staying in the moment." Staying in the moment means that what's important is what *is*, right now, right here. The temptation to think back or project forward is great, but "now" is the focus of your attention. Locking in on your breathing, the most consistent and reliable manifestation of "now," helps you stay in, and be mindful of, the moment. Ironically, kids are almost always much more "in the moment" than their parents—what matters to young kids is what's happening this minute, not what happened yesterday or is scheduled for tomorrow. As noted elsewhere in Part 1 of this book (see the earlier chapter "3D Parenting," and the next chapter, "Listening"), that "now" attribute of kids comes in very handy in resolving many of their crises du jour.

So, how does mindful meditation apply to *No Regrets Parenting?* Taking a deep, settling breath during parenthood's chaos is always a good idea, but when you are with your kids, you can't simply tune everything out and focus on breathing while your kids are desperately asking for ice cream, advice, or the potty. But what you can do is a "parenting meditation" that requires a similar kind of focus. During the precious moments that you have protected to share with your kids, focus on seeing them, hearing them, understanding them, and being amazed by them. I mean *really* seeing every feature of them; *really* hearing every word they say and the tones they say it with; *really* understanding their hopes and wishes and concerns; and *really* being amazed by what you've created—living, breathing miracles of nature who are learning like sponges and growing like weeds. Stay in the moment when you have moments with your kids. During those often too brief interludes, your kids should be all that's happening and where it's at.

For some of you, this will mean really *noticing* your kids for the first time in weeks or months, maybe since the day you held them with awe in the delivery room. At the moment of their birth, they had your undivided attention. You registered every coo, cry, and gurgle; counted their fingers and toes; brushed their wispy hair with your fingers; and kissed them gently on their soft spots. At other momentous occasions, you probably paid pretty close attention, too. Her christening or his bris. The first day of preschool or kindergarten. The first steps they took or the first time balancing on a two-wheeler.

But how will you feel someday if the *next* time you really notice your child is at high school graduation, or on his wedding day? Stunned that it went by so quickly, puzzled by how you missed it even though you were there? Those are regrets; your job is to reach that day with *No Regrets*. That requires paying attention to your kids on all the days in between the big occasions. Noticing them when you're driving them to school, when you read their bedtime story, while you're running through a rainstorm with them or building a snowman. What are your kids thinking? What are they asking? How did they get so cute and so smart?

Be "mindful" of your kids, and be dazzled by them. "Meditate" on their loose teeth and their skinned knees. Marvel as they play baseball or the piano. Be overcome with wonder at their wisdom and innocence.

It is only by *noticing* your children that you will truly *know* your children.

Listening

If you don't listen to your kids, really listen, your time together is wasted. Kids have silly worries and stupid ideas. Kids are immature and repetitive. Impulsive and emotional. They exaggerate and fabricate; they make mountains out of molehills. That may be the way you sometimes hear them, with *your* ears and *your* brain. But your kids think they are wise and insightful, mature, patient, and brilliant. Kids ask questions because they want answers—and because they want your attention. They want to hear you speak to them and teach them. Most important, kids are usually "in the moment" and believe that their issues and concerns, right this minute, are the most important things in the world (see the previous chapter). The mean thing her best friend said; his teacher's unreasonable new rules; the shove he got from the cute girl on the playground; the Valentine's note she wants to leave for her secret crush; the embarrassment he felt when you scolded him in front of his friends. As trite and nonurgent as these matters may sound to your adult ears and brain, they are front-page news for your kids.

Listen to your kids and treat their words with respect. Don't form your response in your head before you've heard their whole saga—if you do, you're not really listening. Let your kids know by your facial expressions, your patience, and your thoughtful response that you feel their pain and share their concerns. Don't ever make your kids feel that you think their worries are trivial. Don't tell your kids they'll understand how minor their issues are when they get older. Parent your kids, don't patronize them. While *you* know that by tomorrow, and maybe even by later tonight, the crisis du jour will have faded, *they* don't know that. Help them get through their crises as you would hope your spouse or close friend would help you get through yours. In this way, you will let your kids know that they can come to you when they're troubled, no matter the nature of the distress, and that you will be there for them. You're their closest friend. They won't have to go elsewhere for comfort, landing in the hands of people who love them a lot less than you do. You're always there, and your kids' problems are your problems, and you will solve them together. Then your kids will include you in their lives and in their bigger crises as they get older.

Our kids seemed to always remember their biggest crises as soon as we pulled into the school parking lot in the morning. As other kids were bounding out of cars all around us, there was always something *really* important that one or more of our kids needed to discuss. They had forgotten to tell us about the test today. Or to study for it. They had forgotten their homework at home. Or their lunch. Or that it was "silly hat day." Or that it *wasn't* "paint your face day." Oops. With the school bell about to ring, or when you're late for work, or when you're exhausted after a long day, it is hard to listen. But that's when you have to try the hardest to lock into your kids' soliloquies. They may be impossible to deal with right now—after all, the BELL *IS* RINGING, or YOU *ARE* LATE FOR WORK! But give your kids your solemn pledge that you will listen, and you will have time tonight. Promise that you will listen to the whole story, beginning to end, as soon as you can. And if your kids know that you do keep your promises to listen to them, and you do think that what they say is important, they will give you a pass until later.

NOW GET OUT OF THE CAR AND INTO SCHOOL!!! Please ☺.

Listening well to your kids has two other big perks, one obvious and one a bit more subtle. The obvious benefit is that you'll know what's going on in their brains and in their lives. We well remember the first time our kids came home from preschool with ideas of their own, notions they dreamed up without our planting them in their heads. Wow, what a revelation it is to hear your kids' original thoughts! As they grow older, their own thoughts and ideas come fast and furiously. They learn from teachers, friends, TV, the Internet. Before you know it, you can lose track of what they're doing and what they're thinking about. Knowing your kids, really knowing them, requires patient listening. And it's by really knowing your kids that you will feel *No Regrets* as the years streak by.

The more subtle benefit to careful listening is the perception you leave with your kids. The actual advice you give is often less important to them, and to the situation at hand, than is the true impression they will form of you: that you care about them and their predicaments. The solution you might offer to any dilemma is rarely as important as the fact you were there to work it through with them. That's like a no-fault guarantee. Even if you blow it, your kids know you gave it your best shot. That in and of itself is a nice lesson for them: Mom and Dad are human and may not always be right, but they tried to help me and were humble enough to admit when their advice was wrong or didn't work. You score big points for effort.

STAYING SANE

This is by way of personal confession and full disclosure: It's not always easy and it's not always enjoyable to be with your kids. Depending on their ages, kids can be physically taxing and emotionally trying (hence the "long days" part of "long days, short years"). Part 2 of this book provides strategies for maximizing the time you have with your kids during your daily routine, before they grow up and leave your daily routine. Tips for squeezing in precious moments while you still can. On the other hand . . . when kids drive you nuts, they can really drive you nuts! So, how to find the right prescription for wonderful and plentiful time with your kids, without overdosing?

Here are four secrets to maintaining your balance:

1. **DOUBLE DIP.** Pick activities that you and the kids would enjoy *without* each other, then do them together. Moviemakers have figured this out and found it to be very profitable; today's slick animated films are targeted to both adult and kid sensibilities. Some of the jokes are way above a child's head, and the story lines may be, as well, but there are also enough cute characters, goofy gags, and slapstick to tickle a wide range of childhood maturity levels. Two hours in the theater with your kids, everyone laughing (albeit, often at different times), everyone sharing popcorn, and everyone talking about the movie in the car on the way home. A great double dip.

Many more activities to keep you and your kids happy at the same time fill Part 2 of this book. A few examples:

Biking—Put the littlest ones in a trailer, the somewhat older ones on a trailer cycle that hooks onto your bike and lets your child pedal; once kids are old enough to bike next to you, they get their own wheels. You get outdoor exercise, your kids get fresh air, and you get each other.

Charity—Do a charity walk together; get sponsors and spend a weekend day doing a healthy outdoor activity for a good cause. Or have a spring-cleaning day during which everyone collects clothes and toys from the closets and under the beds to donate. Then go to the collection center together and show your kids the act of giving.

Jogging—Strollers made for keeping your kids close while you're pounding the pavement are perfect for together times that relieve, rather than create, stress.

Language lessons—Learn a second language together, listening to tapes on long car rides or in the dentist's waiting room.

Swimming—The pool feels great on a hot day whether you're an adult or a kid. When the kids are old enough to play in the pool unsupervised, you can swim laps while they splash their friends.

Reading—Books are one of the best ways to reconcile different attention levels and interests. Quiet time with everyone reading his or her own latest page-turner.

Snow shoveling and leaf raking—Depending on the age of your kids, you may be doing most of the shoveling while you help them build a snowman, make snow angels, or have a snowball fight. The idea is that you're all at the same place at the same time, sharing the experience. And the snow gets shoveled. Same idea with raking the leaves; you rake, the kids play in the piles and help you fill the bags. As the kids get older, of course, feel free to assign them the harder parts of this partnership.

2. **TAKE ADVANTAGE OF *THEIR* COMMITMENTS.** When the kids have activities that you can't share, use that time to escape from parenting and indulge yourself. Beginning with pre-school, your kids' calendars start to fill up with blocks of hours to which you're not invited. These are vital growth opportunities for your kids—and for you! You've earned quality *adult* time and should feel no guilt taking that time for yourself when the kids are doing their thing. Sit in a coffee shop, go to the gym, watch your soap opera, take a bath, sneak in a rendezvous with your spouse. The more you enjoy your time away from the kids, the less you'll feel burdened when you're all together again.

3. **PUT YOURSELF IN "TIME OUT."** Don't feel compelled to share *every* precious moment with the kids. When you've had enough, take a grown-up break and put the kids in front of the TV or take them to Grandma's. Forcing yourself into nonstop togetherness with your kids will spoil them and may spoil your relationship with them. Absence, in limited quantities, can indeed make the heart grow fonder. Spend as much time as you can with your kids, but know when you need a breather, and take it. You're not a bad parent because your kids are watching *Mary Poppins* for the fortieth time. This

is especially important when your temper is about to flare, which it inevitably will do on occasion. Separate yourself from your kids until you're ready to calmly and comfortably reconnect.

4. **BE REALISTIC AND PACE YOURSELF.** If you try to do each and every one of the suggestions in Part 2 of this book, sanity is out of the question. You'll drive yourself and your kids up a wall if you use this book as an inflexible instruction manual for your lives. Rather, see this as a potpourri of ideas, some to try now, others for later; some may never be right for you and your family. You know the chemistry and physics of your household. If summer sleepaway camp is a mainstay for your family, ignore my advice for day camping. If you live in Manhattan, pajama walks after dinner (and during rush hour!) may be a stupid idea. Don't be a room parent or teacher's helper if your middle school kids are mortified by the thought of their friends seeing you in their classrooms. Pick and choose from the menu of together times that make up this book and you'll stay sane while still capturing precious moments with your kids that would otherwise be lost.

Money

Sure, it helps. But there's nothing in this book that requires lots of money. In fact, every chapter in Part 2 can be tailored to your budget without detracting from the fun or fond memories. If the economy is in the potty, or your bank accounts are in recession, your discretionary money for travel, recreation, vacations, and restaurants may vanish. In addition, many parents find themselves scrambling to find extra work, extra sources of income to cover the costs that come with kids. That's potentially a perfect storm for disrupting your time with your kids—more time spent at work and less money to use during nonwork time. It's times like those that test your creativity and ingenuity. This book is written to help you find the most creative and ingenious uses for both your time and your money.

Most of the suggestions for stretching the time with your kids are entirely free—they just need you. Anything in Part 2 that requires *any* money at all can be easily scaled to your means—your favorite family restaurant can be the fast food place, the pancake place, or a more upscale establishment, depending on the priorities you set for family funds. To my mind, the cheaper and healthier the better. You may prefer family movie night to mean a trip to the theater at $10 per ticket—but the $1 video rental from the dispensing box in the supermarket is just as special as long as you're all there together.

One of the biggest mistakes you can make as a parent is to equate, in your own mind or in your kids' minds, the cost of a good time with the good time itself. It would be great if we could all afford the $40 ticket to see the latest kids' musical theater or ice skating extravaganza that comes to town. But if you can't, wait till the free theater-in-the-park programs start next summer, or rent the movie version of the play. If the cost of seeing the hottest teen sensation in concert is prohibitive, record her next TV concert and watch with your kids. And if you *can* afford the tickets for musical theater, the ice skating extravaganza, or the big concert, think twice about whether those are investments you should make; if they are, enjoy them to the fullest. But make sure your kids know these are rare treats, because there are many important things you need to save for, and many worthwhile causes to which you want to donate.

If you don't invest the time and effort to know your kids and to be an integral part of their lives, don't try to buy them off with expensive outings and activities—it won't work. The worst message you can send your kids is that you consider an expensive day out as an offset for the many inexpensive opportunities to be with them that you've missed (see Part 1, "'Quality' vs. 'Quantity' Time"). Not only do you lose your irreplaceable time with them, but you also degrade their value systems about what's important in life.

Beware the "Tiger Mom"
and the "Potpourri Parent"

This is a book about protecting precious moments and redefining quality time with your kids. It's a book about sifting through the responsibilities and commitments of everyday life and reclaiming more time to spend with your kids. Enough time to become an integral part of their lives, and enough time to make them the focal point of your life. But there are potential hazards that come with interwoven lives. If you're not mindful, you might misuse the time you've worked so hard to salvage.

As the product of immigrant parents and grandparents, I know firsthand a culture that drives its young toward overachievement and a mentality that strives for generational advancement—greater success for their kids than parents could have hoped to attain for themselves. The recently coined term "tiger mother" (by author Amy Chua)* is not a new parenting phenomenon, nor is it unique to immigrant families. Über-parenting takes many forms. While it may be true that, as argued by Chua, Chinese immigrant parents pressure their kids toward academic and musical accomplishments, I maintain that American-born Baby Boomers, Generation Xers, and Generation Yers have their own hyperbolic version of child raising, for which I'll coin my own new term: "potpourri parents."

The kids of Boomers, Xers, and Yers are exposed to unprecedented opportunities for self-discovery and mentored accomplishments,

---

* Amy Chua, *Battle Hymn of the Tiger Mother* (New York: Penguin Press, 2011).

in the hope that somewhere in the smorgasbord they will have an experiential epiphany, a sudden realization of their purpose and place. Potpourri kids have karate Mondays and tap dancing Tuesdays; play competitive tennis on Wednesdays (under the supervision of the club pro); get math tutoring after school on Thursday; and have rehearsals for the school play on Friday. Without the inconvenience of school to worry about, weekends are even more ambitiously choreographed. Pushing their kids toward excellence, even superiority—in school, sports, music, theater, standardized tests, etc.—tiger moms and potpourri parents may neglect one of the most important obligations and thrills of parenting: letting kids be kids. The goal of *No Regrets Parenting* isn't limited to its benefits for parents. Kids must also be able to look back on their own childhoods without the regrets of growing up too fast, prematurely feeling adult pressures, and not having enough freedom to be kids.

Teach your kids that ambition is good but that disappointments occur despite trying hard. Encourage them to be the best they can be in everything they do, but let them know they don't necessarily have to be better than everyone else in everything they do. Role model for them— show them your own creativity, enterprise, and passion. But also show them you can have fun. Never lose the joy of parenting, the fraternity and friendship with your kids, or the belly laughs and silliness.

There is no question that tiger moms and potpourri parents love their children dearly and have their kids' best interests at heart. They devote so much of their time and energy toward enhancing their kids. Tiger moms and potpourri parents are fiercely competitive, applying for spots in the most prestigious preschools before their babies are even born. They will tell you how much they enjoy being parents, that they have fun watching their kids discover inner excellence, unmask hidden talents, mature into successful young adults. But take a careful look at some of those parents at spelling bees, Little League tournaments, debate competitions, piano recitals, and swim meets. Do they *look* like they are having fun? More important, watch their kids. Do *they* look like they're having fun?

In an earlier chapter ("The Checkered History of Parenting Advice"), I promised not to delve too deeply into the myriad parenting philosophies that have come and gone and, in some cases, come back again. So here's the condensed version: Find balance. Motivate your kids, but don't forget to giggle with them. Mix study time with downtime, goal setting with ice cream sundaes. As parents, we all share one important fact of life: Our kids grow up too fast. It is true that if we don't push our kids hard enough, they may miss getting the inspiration, structure, and mentoring they need from us. But it is equally true that if we push too hard, our kids may miss being kids, we will miss the delight of watching them be kids, and we will lose the chance to be a bit of a kid ourselves when we're with them.

Find the balance so you'll have *No Regrets* about how you spent the irreplaceable time you have with your kids.

And now, move on to Part 2 for the practical advice: how to find the time you need with your kids, and how to make the most of the time you find.

PART 2

No Regrets Parenting
Simple Strategies

Calendars

Their "Week at a Glance"

The truest measure of you as a person may be your calendar. Yes, the one that sits on your desk, beeps from your smartphone, or pops up on your computer monitor. The choices and commitments you make in your daily scheduling reflect the life you live and the priorities you set. If your calendar were to fall into the hands of a stranger, what would all the entries—the notations, meetings, phone calls, and appointments—say about you? Would the stranger reading your calendar recognize how important being a parent is in your life?

Calendars are all about time management. What better place to start managing your time with your kids than with your calendar? What better place to begin *No Regrets Parenting?*

Before you go to sleep each night, update your calendar with what's on tap for your kids tomorrow. Write it down, or type it in. Better yet, sit down with the kids and put their schedule for the whole week on your calendar every Sunday night. When they're young, your kids' schedules are usually more straightforward than yours: day care or school, perhaps followed by an after-school activity, dinner, homework, and bedtime. But as they get older, the choreography of kids' lives can get very, very complex. Make it a point to know where your kids are and what they're doing.

There are compelling reasons for putting your kids' schedules on your calendar. First, it's nice to know what's going on in your kids' lives. When you are in touch with their activities, you never lose touch with what is important to them. Your conversations with your kids at dinner, at bedtime, and in car pool are all more meaningful if you can talk with them about their day. Glance at your calendar before dinner tonight to remind yourself of what was on the kids' agenda today.

Second, there may be important activities in your kids' days that you should not miss. It's painful to find out about the class presentation or school assembly that you could have fit into your schedule if you had only known about it. Or that your little goalie blocked eight shots in a soccer game you only found out about after it was over. Of course, you still have to work (to afford to enroll your kids in soccer!), and it's very likely that you won't be able to get to all or even many of your kids' events—but if you don't know about them, you won't get to any of them. And you may get a pleasant surprise—one of your meetings is canceled that had conflicted with your child's after-school basketball game! Because the game is on your calendar, you're reminded that if you hurry, you can get there just in time to watch the second half.

Third, knowing where your kids are supposed to be throughout their day gives you an early warning system in case they're not where they're supposed to be. Keeping track of your kids' whereabouts is not spying or invading their privacy—it's good parenting.

Finally, and this is the punch line, your kids' daily activities should be your top priorities, and top priorities should be in your calendar. If there is a way to share those moments with them, by showing up at events where parents are invited (and when your kids will not be embarrassed!), that should be your first choice for how to spend your time. The student council campaign speech, diving catch, perfect pirouette, three-point shot, or double axel will never happen again, at least not exactly the way it did today. Hearing about it afterward is bittersweet when you realize you could have been there.

There are no instant replays in real life.

Major Holidays

*C*hristmas, Passover, birthdays, Thanksgiving, July 4, Mother's Day, Father's Day, and the other Big Days of the year are the perfect occasions for parents to cement lifelong memories for their kids. With the built-in customs and cultures of each holiday as a template, you should personalize each special day with your family's unique imprint. Establish traditions that your kids will look forward to for weeks before the holiday—a special food, a family skit or talent show, a dress-up dinner, decorations, touch football in the backyard, the movie you watch together every year on the same day, an arts-and-crafts afternoon, a fireworks show. And then make sure you and your kids prepare for those rituals together—cooking, baking the cake, rehearsing, picking costumes, decorating, buying supplies.

As wonderful as they can be for bringing family together, major holidays can also be double-edge swords—oftentimes the Big Days involve lots of extended family and friends in the festivities. While it's nice to celebrate with others, make sure you set aside time just for your nuclear crew—a quiet breakfast, hot chocolate together before bed, a walk through the park. When your kids anticipate the upcoming holiday, they should think of the happy times they are going to spend with you, doing things together that all of you do only on that special day each year. And they should look forward to preparing for the rituals of each holiday that are unique to your family.

They will pass those traditions on to their own kids someday, and if you're lucky, they'll invite you to watch the reenactment, now through your eyes as grandparents. What a joy!

Half-Birthdays and Minor Holidays

There is special electricity in the household on holidays. Big Days in the life of the family—birthdays, anniversaries, Mother's Day, Father's Day, Thanksgiving, Christmas—create unique memories and establish lifelong traditions. So, why limit the excuses to celebrate together to a few days a year? You don't need to cook a turkey or give gifts for the kids' half-birthdays, but celebrating half-birthdays gets everyone together for cake and ice cream, or a special dinner or movie night, twice as often.

Declare other family holidays. Observe the first day of school each fall, the last day of school each summer, a good report card, the last of the booster shots at the doctor's office, the first lost tooth, the last lost tooth, your dog's birthday, opening day of baseball season, closing day at the amusement park, the first snowstorm, the first crocus in the garden. Identify those days of the year that have special meaning for your kids and turn those days into events—not major events or major celebrations, not expensive or fancy, just events everyone looks forward to, jokes about, and shares together.

Momentous Moments

our kids' daily activities are hard to squeeze into your own calendar constraints, and you probably will have to miss many of them even if you know about them in advance. But there are certain events you should never miss, lest the years will go by even faster and be more of a blur than they already are. Truth is, especially when your kids are younger, they may not remember whether you were there for each of their "first" events and "big" events. But as you look back, the more of those you've been to, the more you'll feel a part of your child's life. And best of all, today's technology allows you to "be there" even if you can't actually be there.

Never miss the day your child takes her first steps, the first day of kindergarten, the first day riding a two-wheeler without training wheels, the first piano recital, the first day behind the wheel of a real car. Never miss the holiday pageant at school even if your child is just the bunny in the back. Never miss the fifth-grade continuation ceremony or the high school graduation, the first day of Little League or the first day on skis. His first ice skating performance in the big arena, or the first time she swims all the way across the pool.

How can you possibly be there for all of those momentous moments and still keep your job and fulfill your adult responsibilities? One word: video. Ask your spouse, your neighbor, your kids' babysitter, or classmates' parents to record the momentous moments you must miss. Cameras and smartphones that record video are inexpensive enough investments in the life and legacy of your family that you should include one in your budgeting. Amortized over all the important episodes in your kids' growing up, the cost of a basic recording device will be long forgotten, while the joys of experiencing those occasions will last a lifetime.

So, when reality hits and you simply cannot get there, you and your little star can share the moment together afterward as she sits on your lap and narrates the big event for you. Not only does video capture the momentous moments you had to miss, it also lets you send those moments to grandparents, replay them for family movie night, and embarrass her with them at her wedding reception.

Yes, her wedding reception. The years are short indeed.

Weekends

The premise and promise of *No Regrets Parenting* is turning scarce minutes into cherished moments, transforming everyday routines into opportunities for precious time with your kids. So, it may seem a little contradictory to make a big deal out of weekends. They are obviously designed perfectly for together time, and shouldn't even need mention.

But weekends do need mention, as well as careful attention. In the new reality of two–working parent families and, increasingly, two jobs per parent, weekday responsibilities have crept into our weekends. Six- and even seven-day workweeks are not unusual. And although kids' weekends are still protected from school, your kids' programmed activities can quickly consume their weekends, too. Volleyball matches, swim meets, theater practice, baseball tournaments, Sunday school, birthday parties, and playdates—to say nothing of homework—bring Mondays back far too quickly. So quickly that, between your responsibilities and the choreography of your kids' schedules, you may barely see your kids even on weekends. And remember, there are only 940 weekends between your baby's birth and her leaving for college—how many have you already spent rushing past each other on the way to Monday?

For those reasons, all of the suggestions in the coming chapters for squeezing special time with your kids from the hectic weekday chaos—chauffeuring car pool, bedtime rituals, family dinners, pajama walks, sharing chores, family movie nights, etc.—apply equally well to hectic weekends.

Don't take weekend time for granted and don't assume that you and your kids will find one another without advance planning. Synchronize your weekend calendar with your kids with the same rigor and vigor that you apply to coordinating your weekday calendars. There are many more options for family activities with a two-hour chunk of time on a weekend than with a half-hour slot on weekdays; plan ahead and be creative with those options.

Of course, if you and your kids are fortunate enough to have even bigger blocks of time available on weekends, reminiscent of a simpler time, take full advantage. Day trips to the state park, long bike rides, an outing to the amusement park, a college or professional sporting event, the museum, a day with the family on the golf course or at the lake, etc. The beauty of weekends, if you and your kids actually have time off, is that you don't have to squeeze activities into precious moments—you can luxuriate in activities that keep you together for several hours at a time. Your kids will feel the difference. The calm that comes with unhurried hours, versus the pressure that comes with scarce minutes, is rejuvenating and makes Monday more bearable.

Sleep

Pajama Walks

The hour before bedtime can be chaotic with young kids. There is lots of advice out there but little real science addressing the best ways to calm and quiet the kids before tucking them in. One of my favorite techniques, weather permitting, is a pre-bedtime pajama walk. Not only does it give kids gentle, tranquil moments to decompress from their hyper after-dinner activities, but it also gives parents special moments with their kids that otherwise might have been lost to TV.

The key to pajama walks is the pajamas. Get the kids completely ready for bed—teeth brushed, faces washed, pajamas on. Then put them in their strollers, or on their tricycles, or in their sneakers, and meander slowly around the neighborhood. No snacks en route (their teeth are already brushed!); don't kick the soccer ball along the way or bring the baseball mitts; postpone animated conversations until tomorrow. These are the mellow moments.

It may take a couple laps, but by the time you arrive back home with your kids, they will be in a fresh-air trance and ready for bed; they may even fall asleep on the way, and just need your tender transfer into the house and under the covers.

The "La-La Song"

*Y*our kids are never more angelic, never more serene, and never cuddlier than in the moments before they go to sleep. That is, of course, after you've survived the crescendo that builds right before bedtime, the protests about not being tired, the three glasses of water, and the last-minute homework panic.

Bedtime rituals give kids a sense of security and stability. When you are part of those rituals, your presence becomes fixed in your children's minds, associated with the tranquility and comfort of their beds and their good dreams. Establish a ritual, and be there to participate in it. It may be a pajama walk (see the previous chapter). It may be a lullaby, a story (see the next chapter), a chat about the day just passed, a prayer, or just a few minutes of holding each other. Our ritual was a bedtime story followed by the "La-La Song"; we replaced the words of an old folk song, popular before the kids were born, with la-las. We la-la'ed the same tune every night, in a soft voice, while holding them or lying next to them. Soon the "La-La Song" became our family's comfort song. Anytime of the day, whenever the kids were upset or frightened, we'd la-la them until the crisis passed.

There are seven nights in a week—plan to be there at bedtime for most of them, even if it means going back to the office some nights. When your kids get older, the rituals may change. Your adolescents may just want a kiss on the cheek as *you* go to bed because they are still doing homework. Or in the summer, it may just be a phone call to say goodnight because your teens are out later than *your* bedtime. But you should be part of every bedtime at every age.

Trust me—when they're away at college or on their own and their beds are empty, you'll miss those bedtime traditions. Don't miss them when the kids are still home.

Story Time

There are so many good things to say about bedtime stories. From just a few months of age up until the "middle age" years—at least seven, eight, or nine—kids love stories almost as much as parents love reading or telling them. There were some books that we read hundreds (hundreds!) of times to our kids as they were growing up. We knew every word by heart. There were times when our kids had to remind us to turn the page because we were reciting the story from memory and our minds had wandered mid-paragraph.

Story time can be so much more than reading storybooks to your kids. Make up stories where there's no book. Use puppets (socks work just fine). If you can draw, illustrate the story as you're making it up. If you can sing, sing the story. Tell stories of your own life, funny and moving things that happened when you were a child, or what your parents taught you, and where they took you. Use story time to make your life before having kids a vibrant image in your kids' minds. How I met Daddy, how pretty Mommy looked when I saw her for the first time, what the army was like, your college roommate's funny habits, and the weird people in your dorm. Old yearbooks make great story time material. Use your wedding album, or photo albums of your kids when they were babies or too young to remember their outings. Tell them about their adventures when they were little and how funny it was when they got scared by the raccoon at the campsite, when they got stuck at the top of the Ferris wheel, or when they sat on a horse for the first time. (Our oldest child never tired of the true story, with pictorial proof, of his first real horseback ride, when everyone else got horses with macho names like Lightning, Thunder, Blaze, and Cannon, but he got Lumpy. He still laughs when we remind him!) Use a world atlas to tell your kids bedtime stories about faraway countries you've visited or read about, or how the oceans are all connected; show them where the Eskimos live.

Leave plenty of time before lights out for an unhurried, leisurely tale. Bedtime stories should never feel rushed, no matter how desperate you are to have some quiet adult time before your own bedtime—even if it means you have to stay up a little later yourself. You will be rewarded by having your kids start to request their favorite stories—"Tell the one about how Grandpa took you to the rodeo and you won a ribbon," or "Tell me about the night you first took Mommy to the movies," or "Tell me about the Eskimos again." How great is that?!

Sleepless Sleepovers

I have never figured out what it is about sleepovers that kids love so much. Anyone of voting age knows that a night slept in your own bed is a guarantee of a better night's sleep than one spent anywhere else. Certainly no right-minded adult would ever prefer to sleep at a friend's or relative's house unless it was at the bottom of a ski mountain or overlooking the ocean.

Yet, kids of all ages, even teenagers who should know better, still want to sleep at friends' houses. Probably has something to do with lax rules and late bedtimes. Very little actual sleeping occurs at sleepovers. Come to think of it, maybe it's best we don't exactly understand the appeal of sleepovers. But we should take advantage of it. Make your house the preferred sleepover destination. Serve the best snacks, show the best movies, prepare the best pancake breakfasts. Having your kids' friends spend time at your house gives you a wonderful window into the relationships your kids have and into the lives of the friends your kids hang with. There's also the control feature—you're in charge of the movies they watch and the bedtime they keep. You make sure they brush their teeth and wash their faces. You can peek in on the activity and eavesdrop on the conversations. You can even sneak a goodnight kiss when none of their friends is looking.

Although it's easier to ship the kids elsewhere than it is to host a houseful, the more time they sleep away, the less time you get to see them in their element, and the fewer goodnight kisses you get. And when your kids sleep elsewhere, some other kid's parents get to spy on your kids—who knows what your child may say to totally embarrass you!

But as hard as you try to win the "Sleepover House of the Year Award," you won't always get to be the host—your kids will want a turn elsewhere, and other parents may be reading this book, too, vying for host honors. Although sending your kids to a friend's house for a sleepover does little to deepen your insight into your kids' lives, it's not all bad, either. Sleeping at a friend's house builds your child's self-confidence and independence; it prepares her for school trips, sleepaway camp, and, ultimately, college. So don't feel guilty when your kids have a great time at an away sleepover; they will grow from the experience. Learn what made it fun for them, and steal the best ideas for your next sleepover event.

It's time to invest a few bucks and buy an air mattress or two for your new house guests.

While They Were Sleeping

Among the most common complaints of parenthood is the diametrically opposite sleep habits that kids have compared with adults. Very young kids go to bed early and wake early; older kids stay up much too late and sleep past noon. But, although frustrating at times (especially when toddlers are ready to roll at 6 A.M. and teens are just rolling in at midnight), the differences in sleep schedules between you and your kids present the perfect ploy for balancing your work hours with the hours you want to spend with your kids.

When your kids are young, schedule more work in the evenings, after they've gone to bed; when your kids are older, use the early morning hours to work when they're still sleeping. Nap time, Mother Nature's glorious gift to parents of young children, presents additional opportunities for sneaking adult productivity into life with kids.

Of course, not all work time is flexible. Punch clocks and teleconferences can't be manipulated around bedtimes and nap times. But work that can be shifted should be—housework, take-home reading, e-mail responses, Internet research, and other tasks that spill over from your regular work schedules are prime candidates for creative rescheduling. As great a temptation as it is to take advantage of finally getting everyone to sleep for some well-deserved downtime for yourself, this is a chance to reprogram your idea of downtime into the concept of together time. If you can get some of your work done while they are asleep, you'll be able to spare more time from work when your kids are awake.

Yes, you still need downtime, away from the kids, to collect yourself and find balance. Fortunately, kids at all ages sleep a lot longer than you do, meaning you can squeeze in a couple hours of work and still have time for your own repose.

School

Homework Helper

This is a tricky one. You already went through third grade yourself; now it's your child's turn and you shouldn't be the one doing "times tables." But . . . you should know that your child is doing times tables, should look over her homework after it's finished every night, and should be there to help just in case 4 times 8 becomes 24. Homework checking time is a wonderful opportunity to sit close to your child, maybe while he's in pajamas and maybe with a cup of cocoa, and provide positive reinforcement for a job well done—or constructive advice on how to do it better tomorrow night. Homework helps kids build independence and learn to take responsibility, so don't feel that you have to compulsively check each math problem or spelling lesson for minor mistakes—that's not the point of homework helping. The point is that this is a valuable together time with your kids, and it shows them that homework matters to you and should matter to them.

Don't just ask, "Finish your homework?" and wait for the inevitable (and exasperated) *"Yessss,* Dad!" Make it a ritual to have your kids show you the finished product—not because you don't trust them, and not because you're worried about the dangling participle they may have missed, but because you are proud of the work they do and it makes you happy to see them doing such a nice job. Your pride in their work will become their pride in their own work.

How long should this ritual go on? Through middle school. By high school, your kids will have gotten all the right messages from you about homework, and then will be ready for the autonomy that brings with it the nightly question from outside the closed bedroom door: "Finish your homework?" (*"Yessss*, Dad!")

High school doesn't mean you stop reinforcing the importance of homework; it just means you don't cuddle up every night and see the actual workbook pages. But stay in touch: Ask your teenagers how their homework grades are, and ask them to show you the comments written by teachers on the graded homework. That gives you ongoing opportunities for praise and pride. And make sure your high schoolers know you are available to help with their homework if they ask for help. That assumes, of course, that by the time your kids are in high school you can still understand their schoolwork well enough to help.

Science Fair and "Super" Homework

*N*ot all homework is equal. Some school assignments warrant more of your direct, hands-on help than others. These are the big projects—like the dreaded dioramas, nature-collection wall posters (butterflies, biomes, mushrooms, pinecones, seashells, etc.), life-size models of the solar system, and Popsicle-stick bridge-building contests. Even though your house looks like it may never recover from the assault of construction paper, superglue, and pine needles, and you are exhausted from the late-night runs to the hardware store or hobby shop, you should look forward to "super" homework assignments. They offer special moments of teamwork between you and your kids, with an important twist—in these collaborations, your children are the team leaders and you are the assistant. If you forget that it's their projects, you'll lose the uniqueness of the time together and you will send the wrong message about taking responsibility.

Preparing for a science fair is a wonderful example of "super" homework together time. The moments you and your kids spend confirming the existence of gravity, determining the tensile strength of steel, assessing age and gender determinants of memory, or predicting the particle distribution of potential biological warfare agents can be priceless quality time together. Since it's unlikely that you are already an expert in any of those subjects, you and your child will learn together. You teach her how to research a subject, think about which questions to ask, and design a research plan to answer those questions.

Don't panic. Of course, the teachers at school will lay the foundation and establish the rules and guidelines to follow for the big project. But parental involvement is welcomed by most teachers, if for no other reason than to prevent the kids from burning down the house. For these "super" homework assignments, even though you've already been through middle school yourself (see the previous chapter), you get to work more closely and be more helpful than would be appropriate for nightly math or social studies homework.

Your kids need your help, their teachers encourage it, and you get meaningful and memorable time with your kids. Super!

Book Club

Teach your kids to love reading while involving yourself in *what* they're reading. Routinely ask them what they think about what they read. When your kids are assigned a book to read for school, you should read it, too. Or at least skim through it. At the same time, and at the same pace. Sometimes this may mean that you need two copies of the book (that's what libraries are for); usually you just pick up the book when your kids put it down to do other homework.

Though reading the books your children are reading for school isn't always a stimulating experience for you, it does give you valuable insight into their world. But don't stop there. Your kids should be reading books for pleasure, not just because of a school assignment. Here's another way to "double dip" (one of the "Staying Sane" strategies in Part 1 of this book) while parenting: When your kids are reading their fun books, you can be reading your fun books at the same time, in the same room, with the same bowl of popcorn or pot of hot apple cider. Reading defies age and avoids the tedium that sometimes comes with trying too hard to spend every minute with your kids doing kid activities. Seeing you read, like everything else your kids subconsciously study about you, tells kids that reading is important to you and should be important to them.

Reading skills correlate better than any other metric with success in college and beyond. When your kids are young and impressionable, teach them to love reading by reading with them. Our kids have brought books home from college for us to read because they thought we would enjoy them as much as they did. For a parent, that's really coming full circle.

Room Parents and School Volunteers

Few adult volunteer activities are more productive, more necessary, and more welcome than those available at your kids' school. Every school, public and private, is underfunded and shorthanded. The school can use your help. Regularly spending part of a school day at your kids' school gives you an up close look at what your kids see—their teachers and friends, hallway dynamics, and locker lore. For some, being a room parent is ideal—working closely with the teachers and other parents for school programs, fund-raising, field trips, etc. For others, it may be volunteering in the office or lunchroom, hallway monitoring, or standing on the corner as a crossing guard. Drive for field trips, keep the scorebook at basketball or baseball games, chaperone class social events, be the "cast mom" for the school play or the assistant coach/helper dad for the track team. It's valuable to get to know your kids' schoolmates and the other parents. When you have experienced the context of their school lives, your dinner conversations and carpool rides become more interesting and relevant for you and for your kids. You know their turf and even speak their language a little better. More important, you also gain a clearer understanding of your kids' worries and phobias, fallouts with friends, and playground gossip; these insights all pay dividends when your kids come to you for advice.

There's another benefit to volunteering at school. When you volunteer, the teachers and the principal know you are an involved and committed parent. Kids of involved and committed parents get a little extra attention, and parents get a slightly earlier warning if concerns arise about their kids. It's not a calculated or planned benefit for parent volunteers, and certainly not one that is promoted or that teachers will even admit to, but when you're around the school more, the opportunities for interacting with your kids' teachers are increased, and everyone knows you are "watching." Ask most teachers what they most hope for at the start of every school year and they'll tell you—involved parents.

As there are special benefits, there is also a noteworthy downside to school volunteer work—it may absolutely mortify your kids for their friends to see you hanging around the school. When your kids are young, seeing you in the hallway is usually a thrill for them and they run to give you a hug. But as they get a little more socially aware, your presence becomes more chilling than thrilling. Be sensitive to your kids' feelings about this—if your being at the school embarrasses your kids, find a way to stay close but from a safe distance. Work on the school newsletter or help design the school Web page from your home office, spend a few weekend hours at the school helping the teachers or administrative staff catch up on test grading or other paperwork, plan the sports banquet or teacher appreciation day, volunteer with the school's after-hours program for working parents.

That pit-in-your-stomach feeling about how fast your kids are growing up, the one you get each time your children finish another year in school ("How in the world can third grade already be over?!"), will ease a little if you've shared a part of their school experiences.

Back-to-School Nights and Parent–Teacher Conferences

*D*on't miss any opportunities to hear about what's going on in school, and especially what's going on with your kids in their classrooms. The more you know about school, the better able you are to share the learning experience with your kids. Early in the school year, back-to-school nights give you a chance to hear about changes in the curriculum, meet new teachers and staff, and tour the facilities. After some weeks or months, parent–teacher conferences put you and your kids' teachers face-to-face to discuss your kids' performance and progress in the classroom.

If you're reading this book, I don't have to convince you how important it is to keep your finger on the pulse of your kids' schoolwork. But, as with everything else in these chapters, back-to-school nights and parent–teacher conferences bring the added benefit of quality moments with your kids. Though it's true that kids typically don't accompany you to school for these events, the fun begins when you get home. There are few things about school that kids enjoy (or fear!) more than hearing what their teachers said about them and what you think about their teachers. The time you spend with your kids "debriefing" after the parent–teacher conference is fun, gossipy, and very practical—you get to tell them what they are doing right and what they could be doing better at school, and they get a chance to respond. This all sets a great tone for your ongoing involvement in your kids' educations. And kids learn even more from these discussions. They learn that teachers are human, can be approached and spoken to, and want kids to succeed. Seeing that you are not intimidated by talking to teachers, and learning from you how to do so respectfully, establishes a template for your kids to feel comfortable discussing schoolwork with their teachers as partners in the learning process—a skill that will play well when they head off to college and avail themselves of professors' office hours for help and advice. Parents and teachers are typically the most important authority figures in a child's life. When those authority figures get together to talk about that child, it's big news that's worth sharing.

Occasionally a more dramatic intervention into your kids' parent–teacher relationships may be needed. If your child is struggling in a class or you suspect the dynamic between the teacher and your child is strained, you might consider scheduling a cameo appearance during actual class hours. Sitting in the back of the classroom can give you an unparalleled perspective for reconciling your child's version of events that you heard at dinner with the teacher's version that you heard at parent–teacher conferences or via a call from the principal. Your being in the room, during class, serves multiple purposes. You put your child on notice that this is the real deal, that you are taking a day off from work, and that you are even willing to risk potential embarrassment to your child to get to the bottom of the problem. You also show the teacher that this is the real deal—that you are engaged, an activist in your child's education. It puts both your child and her teacher on their best behaviors, at least for the day; but often there is a carryover when both parties know you might be back. Avoid the temptation to automatically side with your child and blame the teacher. Though, in your child's eyes, that would make you his best friend, it isn't parenting. In most situations, the teacher has identified a real problem with your child's learning or behavior that needs to be solved, and you will have a better idea of how to solve it after your visit. But, importantly, there are times when the teacher's behavior may be the problem and, if so, your visit puts you in a much better position to seek a solution for that, as well.

Parent–Teacher–Student Teamwork

*P*TAs, PTOs, and PTSOs are vital to a school's health. They do not, per se, increase the time you have with your kids (unless they, too, are involved as student representatives in the group). In fact, the meetings may take you away from home during homework hours or other family time. But . . . the long-term benefits of active membership in your school's parent–teacher group are substantial, and include many of those associated with school volunteering and room parenting (see the previous chapter). Knowing what's going on at school, showing the teachers that you are an involved parent, and keeping your ear to the ground regarding the school's direction are all invaluable for maximizing your child's classroom experience. The enrichment programs, extracurricular activities, and teacher support functions developed and implemented by parent–teacher organizations help to navigate the school toward shared goals. You will be a better partner in your kids' educations when you invest your time in their school.

But that's not to say that your PTA/PTO/PTSO involvement should exclude your kids. On the contrary, it gives you a great opportunity to share an important experience with them. Tell your kids when you're going to meetings, and ask them for suggestions to bring to the other parents and to the teacher reps. What works in your kids' classrooms and what doesn't? What are the biggest problems with the cafeteria, the gym, the assemblies, or the field trips? Where should fund-raising dollars be directed to have the most benefit for your kids' classes? Including your kids as advisers and allies in your organizational activities lets them know that you respect their opinions enough to ask and to act on them, and gives you yet another way to be your kids' advocate. It's like having your own personal "parent–student organization" at home, complete with its own meetings and refreshments.

College Counseling

Applying to college can be grueling and stressful for kids and their families. Most high schools offer college counseling services to their juniors and seniors; some parents hire private counselors to supplement what the school offers. College counselors help kids with everything from picking the most appropriate schools to apply to, writing personal statements (a.k.a. college essays), choosing which teachers to request recommendation letters from, practicing interview skills, and even deciding what to wear for interviews. Add to the college preparatory medley the standardized-test preparation centers and tutors who charge a hefty fee to help high schoolers improve their SAT and ACT scores; the panoply of books with strategies for nailing your child's dream college that fill the bookstore shelves; and, of course, online counseling services aplenty.

Why would you even consider leaving all this fun to others? But seriously, what's wrong with letting the professionals do all the advising and preparation of your kids for one of the most important milestones in their lives?

There are compelling reasons for you to be an important part of this process, not the least of which is the variable competency of college counselors. But there are the two most important reasons: First, if you have been practicing *No Regrets Parenting* since your kids were little, no one knows them as well as you do; and second, becoming intimately involved in your kids' college commotion can be the best quality time you will ever have with kids at this age. When you add the college application years (sixteen- and seventeen-year-olds) to the driver's ed years (fifteen- and sixteen-year-olds, with whom I will urge your active participation behind the wheel in a later chapter in this book), you can accomplish the near impossible: salvaging many hours and days of quality time with your kids during their busiest and most exciting years, when the competition for their time is greatest. Having these experiences with your adolescents will set the stage for a true *No Regrets* send-off to college.

College applications can be the most captive time you've had with your kids in one place since you moved their playpen into the kitchen seventeen years earlier. Find a way to be an important part of this process. Your role may be as simple as taking your high schooler to your office with you on weekends and having her fill out applications while you catch up on work. Using your office as a "college war room" may help her better focus on the task at hand, with you close by for questions, advice, moral support, and lunch as needed. Or you may choose to become much more engaged in the process.

Pick those parts of the college application process that you feel most comfortable helping with. Maybe it's reading a college listings book with your child, or going online together to the Web sites of schools she's interested in. Set up a chart together for comparing schools by characteristics that are important to her. Use the chart as you would a scavenger-hunt list to negotiate each college's Web site—together find the pieces of information needed to complete the chart, and pause along the way at other pages that look interesting for other reasons. Then use the chart to begin comparison shopping and narrowing down the choices.

Maybe you were good at standardized tests in your day and can help your son study for his. But even if you still get hives thinking about your own SAT, you can "proctor" his practice tests. Tell him when to begin and when it's "pencils down." When he's done with each practice section, go over the answers in the back of the book and help him understand the explanations given for each wrong answer. While he's in the middle of a timed forty-minute section, use that time for your own work or to catch up on e-mails—a rather sober but productive form of the "double dip" strategy for staying sane as a parent, which I described in Part 1 of the book.

Who knows your daughter's life experiences better than you? Brainstorm potential topics for her personal statement, and then help her with the final editing and proofreading. Of course, this must be her essay, but it's common for students to get a little guidance in choosing the topic and editing the final draft; professional college counselors and high school English teachers also help students with their essays. Most colleges require letters of recommendation from teachers; some also accept letters from community contacts your child has had. Go over the pros and cons of potential letter writers together. If you've been practicing *No Regrets Parenting* all along, you know your child's teachers and outside contacts better than any college counselor could.

Financial aid applications are a complicated but essential part of college applications. Often this job falls heavily on parents because they know where their tax forms are stored, but this is a wonderful opportunity to teach your kids the realities of budgets and bank accounts as they relate to tuition, books, room, and board. You can work on the financial aid package while she's writing her personal statement in the "war room" you've set up; then discuss both projects with each other.

Which colleges to apply to is a complex decision that will depend on your particular family dynamics (and on the success of your college savings plan!). A somewhat simpler decision is which colleges to visit during the decision-making process. Whether he ultimately ends up at the community college in town, the state university up north, or the Ivy League school thousands of miles away, a trip together to visit the schools that look especially promising is a memorable way to share this unique time in your kids' lives.

Finally comes the big decision about which college to attend. Now it's time for a family meeting. Gather everyone together to debate the pros and cons of each option. Ultimately, of course, your college applicant gets a bigger say than her siblings. It's your job to frame the discussion with adult perspectives on what's important to look for in a college, and on the financial realities. But everyone should weigh in on big decisions like this because they profoundly affect the whole family.

Looking back, the process won't seem nearly as burdensome as you had feared. And you'll have the immense satisfaction that comes with sharing those precious moments on the eve of her leaving home. Oh my goodness! She's leaving home?!

Don't worry. As you'll read in Part 3 of this book, the Epilogue, there's still a lot of parenting left even after they start college.

Work

A Corner (of Your) Office

I confess. Sometimes it's a relief to go to work. When the frenetic energy at home reaches fever pitch, your office can be the perfect escape. Well, don't get too comfortable. Your office can also be a special escape for your kids who need a change of venue for their big homework project, quiet reading assignment, or special milestone events—like studying for the SAT or filling out college applications (see the previous chapter).

Your office has distinct advantages over the library or a friend's house as a work refuge for your kids. First and foremost, you're there. By reserving a small corner of your work space for your kids, you have found another way to share yourself with them. Your work is no longer a mystery, where you go each day is familiar, and your kids are included in a part of your life they previously could picture only in their minds. Now, when you talk about work at dinner, your kids know what you're talking about.

At your office, your kids know they have to lock in and focus on their own work—you're busy, others around you are busy, and there's no place for distractions. Their efficiency will be high and, hopefully, their presence won't reduce your efficiency—if that happens, they have to know you won't be able to bring them along again.

Finally, your office may be a place where you and your kids can work together. If it's for their special projects, you're close by for the occasional advice or guidance they may need. But they may also be able to help with your work. Really. Depending on your kids' ages, the work you give them to "help" you may be just "make work" to keep them occupied and near you. Draw a picture of Mommy working at her desk to show Grandpa; write as many words with more than three letters as you can for my file on big words; put all the big paper clips in this cup and the little ones in the other cup. But as they get older, your kids can be a real help with filing, data management, answering the phones, fixing the Internet connection, etc. Your kids are probably better techies than you are—make them earn their keep. Real-world rules, however, may make bringing your kids to the office during work hours impractical—you don't want to irritate your coworkers or your boss. If you have access to your workplace off-hours or on weekends, use your work space as a retreat for quiet time with your kids when you or they have projects that spill over from the workweek. Usually you won't meet with objections to having kids with you when you're off the clock. Bring a special lunch or snack with you to make the visits more fun. Make sure you keep pictures of your kids on your desk or bulletin board; when they see their pictures, your kids know you think about them when you're at work and you are proud to show them off to the people you work with.

Going to the office (or store or factory or shipyard) with Mom or Dad is a bigger deal for your kids than you might imagine—and taking them to work will change the way you look at your workplace even when they're not there with you. Who knows? It may even motivate you to clean the place up a bit!

Business Trips and Career Days

Sharing a corner of your office with your kids (see the previous chapter) is not the only way for them to understand what you do for a living and to learn about adult professions and careers.

If you travel a lot for work, pick certain of those trips to take one of your kids along—but only one kid at a time. The experience of a one-parent-one-kid trip is very special for both you and your child, no matter how many kids you have. But if there is more than one child in your home, when else do you get to exclusively focus on, pamper, and take excursions with just one of them? Rotate trips among the kids so each knows that it's his or her turn the next time you can take a child with you.

The kid part of the trip can be almost free—they ride with you in the car or use your frequent flier mileage, and stay in your hotel room; they have to eat whether they are home or on the road with you. But, although not usually financially prohibitive, the logistics can be tricky. Successfully turning a routine business trip into an adventure for both you and your child requires thought and planning.

First, consider the business agenda for the trip; the more flexible your agenda, the better. How long is the trip? Ideally it's long enough to allow for a couple nights in a hotel (as much as you may hate hotels, they are big fun for kids) and for at least a couple memorable excursions after each day's business is finished. What's the venue? Try to pick a business trip that takes you to a fun city. Big cities offer touristy things your kids will remember for a long time. Sure, Disney destinations are great, but visits to theme parks may require more time than a typical business trip allows. But big cities offer lots of simpler expeditions that can be taken after each day's meetings: the elevator ride to the top of the famous skyscraper; a professional sports game; a bike ride across the famous bridge at sunset; or a dress-up theater production or concert. If your meeting locale doesn't offer pizzazz activities like those, find less famous, but still fun, local activities. Community theater, minor league baseball games, county fairs, miniature golf, and go-kart tracks also make for cherished moments and memories. No matter how high the skyscraper elevator climbs, how exciting the sporting event, or how fast the go-karts, it's being with you that your kids will remember most.

Career days at school are like bringing a parent for show and tell. Your kids get to introduce you and be proud of what you do and of how interesting the other kids find you. But it's even more than that—career day can be the most effective way for your kids to understand what you do. Before your appearance in the classroom, rehearse with your child at home. Tell him what you plan to say and ask for advice on how to make it sound cool. Ask him if you should bring along visual aids—rocks if you're a geologist, model rockets if you're a rocket scientist, X-rays if you're a doctor, handcuffs if you're a police officer, a lasso if you're a cowboy. Think of hands-on ways to make your career come alive: Which rocks taste salty, which ones streak red on the sidewalk, and which ones flake and peel? How do the rocket components separate at each stage? Which bone's connected to the head bone? How tight are handcuffs? Who can throw a rope around the teacher? Don't worry if your career isn't as flashy as other parents'. Work with your child to explain how important what you do is—even if the other kids in class aren't dazzled by tax preparation, real estate sales, or bankruptcy law, your own child will have a better appreciation for the contribution you make. The best part of career day is the time you spend with your kids rehearsing your presentation and then talking about it afterward that night at dinner.

Take advantage of any opportunities for your kids to feel part of the life you lead while they're in school. Let them sit in the back row of lectures or presentations you are giving. Include them for company picnics and office outings; sign up for "take your daughter to work day"; bring them to your factory cafeteria for lunch. These are *No Regrets Parenting* moments, quality time that gives your kids a better understanding of who you are.

And a better understanding of where their allowance comes from.

Making Lemonade—Their Office

Kids should start several businesses during their childhood, and teaching them how is a marvelous way for you and your kids to spend time together. It's also a great way to teach them about money, budgets, marketing, public relations, and working with others.

Start with the lemonade stand. My own childhood lemonade business taught me how to address adults as "ma'am" and "sir." It also resulted in my adulthood vow to never drive past a lemonade stand without stopping to buy. I always pay with a dollar bill to see if the kids can make change—and then I give them the change as a tip. Before setting your kids up at the lemonade stand, practice making change with them. Explain overhead and profit. Set a goal for the money your kids will make: teach them about savings, shop ahead for the special purchase they can make when they've earned enough, or identify the charity to which your kids can contribute the earnings. Best idea—do all three. Teach your kids that there are many demands on income and that skillful budgeting can help meet all of those demands—for saving, for buying, and for giving.

Lemonade stands should grow into more sophisticated businesses as your kids grow: lawn mowing, snow shoveling, gardening, babysitting, running a summer "camp" in your backyard for younger kids in the neighborhood. The best part of all of these entrepreneurial ventures that you help your kids undertake is that you are helping your kids undertake them. You are strategizing with them, giving them on-the-job training, sharing their experiences, teaching them life lessons, and watching them grow into junior citizens. And then you get to go to the bank with them, shop with them, and learn with them about the charities they are supporting.

And it all starts with just lemons, water, and a little sugar.

Holding the Flashlight

Never fix a leaky faucet, change a tire, check the oil in the car, paint the fence, or replace the furnace filter while your kids are on Facebook or watching TV. Turn off the computer or TV and turn on the flashlight. You are your kids' source of knowledge for all things handy and practical. Arm them with the flashlight and talk to them all the way through the repairs you're making and the maintenance you're performing. Home improvements are a great way to spend time with your kids while teaching them about tools and life at the same time. The attic, the basement, and the crawl space are all classrooms for learning, and opportunities for sharing. Take advantage of kids' inexplicable love of ladders to coach them in caution and to build trust. For all but the oldest of your helpers, power tools are off limits, of course—but even those weapons of mass construction can be fun for kids, giving them a chance to wear goggles and earplugs at a safe distance while you power up. Please pardon our dust.

As kids get older, *you* should start holding the flashlight for *them*, instructing them on how things work and how to safely fix things that don't work. New tile or countertops, built-in shelves, and paint jobs are bonus chances for time with your kids. Take them to the hardware store with you before the job begins, and then to the ice cream store when the job is finished.

Home

Kitchen (and Laundry) Duty

It is often said that the kitchen is the focal point of the house. It can also be a focal point for time with your kids. As tempting as it may be to put them in front of the TV while you're cooking dinner or cleaning up after meals, don't. There's a lot for kids to do in the kitchen, and lots for them to learn. Start by letting them be the official tasters, and work up to water-glass fillers and table setters. All kids can benefit by being kitchen savvy, and even if it takes a little longer to get dinner on or off the table with all the "help" you're getting from the kids, it's worth it. Not only will your kids learn about healthy food choices, following recipes, cooking, baking, and which side the fork goes on, but they'll also have bragging rights at dinner when everyone says how delicious the meal is. Even more important than the skills they'll pick up there, the kitchen gives you unscripted and unprogrammed time for conversation and sharing. And your kids will have spent important moments with you as a role model, caring and providing for your family.

When the meal is done, your kids are the clean-up crew—again, avoid the temptation to send them away in the name of efficiency. Clean-ups are never as leisurely or interactive as meal preparation, but they do imbue your kids with a sense of nightly responsibility and teamwork. When you let kids run from the table after dinner, you are sending the message that it's your job to serve them, rather than the message that chores are a shared family responsibility. The wrong message here can lead to a sense of entitlement in other aspects of your relationship with your kids. Kids are entitled to your love, your protection, and your mentoring—they are not entitled to your bussing tables, dishwashing, and floor sweeping.

Although no one ever says the laundry room is the focal point of the house, many of the same togetherness benefits accrue while loading the washer, emptying the dryer, folding the clean clothes, and, when your kids are old enough, ironing. The messages to your kids are the same as those from kitchen duty: shared responsibility, no entitlements.

Come into My "Office"

*B*ack in the '60s, there was a popular TV comedy show (recently remade as a movie) called *Get Smart*, about a bumbling but self-assured, and quite lucky, spy who worked for the good guys, an agency named CONTROL. The bad guys spied for KAOS, an evil international organization. Long before anyone had cell phones, our hero, Maxwell Smart, had a "shoe phone" (I guess today they would have called it a "Smart phone." Sorry about that, Chief!) and a "lazer blazer" (laser beams that shot out from his sports coat button). Among the best devices of the show, though, was the "cone of silence," a plastic sheath that enveloped two people who needed ultimate privacy for important secret-agent business. No one outside the cone could hear the important talk going on inside. Predictably, in each episode, the cone helped CONTROL prevail over KAOS.

There should be a special place in every home, no matter how large or small your home may be, where heart-to-heart discussions are held in a "cone of silence." It may be an overstuffed love seat in the family room, a nook in the basement, a corner of the attic, or the rooftop of your apartment building. When your kids have a crisis, real or imagined, say to them, "come into my 'office' and let's talk about it." It may actually even *be* your home office where the tête-à-têtes take place—just make sure you're not sitting behind your desk with your child on the other side.

The point of designating an "office" for important home conversations with your kids is that it's a trusted and safe spot where they can bare their souls in private, and where you can patiently listen. Then you can advise or sympathize, or bare your own soul. This special "office" space should be small enough for one-on-ones, and distinct from where the whole family gathers for the important "shareholder meetings" I describe later in this book.

There's a particular magic for a child knowing that he has your undivided, undistracted attention during times of worry or stress. No one else can enter or interrupt during these "office hours." The meetings often don't last very long, but they almost always end up with a plan, a kiss, and everyone feeling better than they did before the meeting started. CONTROL prevails over KAOS.

Grease Monkeys and Yard Hands

The garage is the most important part of your home that's not actually in the house. Whatever project you are working on in the garage can include your kids—from fixing the car, to tinkering with the lawnmower, to carpentry at your workbench, to sweeping out the mud that came in on the tires. Garages are laboratories, lecture halls, and libraries in your kids' life-skills education; garages are also unhurried venues for one-on-one time with your kids. Think how much more valuable it is for your kids to see you fix an old toy than it is to give them a new toy when the old one breaks—and think about all the different things you can talk about while doing the repairs. Garages hold vital values for kids: self-confidence, self-reliance, inquisitiveness, creativity.

The yard is another learning center for kids. Teach them about plants and flowers, and about saving water. Pull the weeds up by the roots, rake the leaves into a pile big enough to be a trampoline, and clean the gutters before the next rain. Clear the snow off the driveway with two shovels, one large and one small. Most important, listen to your kids' observations, answer their questions, and occasionally sprinkle them with the hose or hit them with a snowball just to keep it silly. At first your kids might prefer video games or their MP3 player to working outdoors, but they'll soon learn from you that heavy leaves in the bag and wet snow on the shovel are the best "downloads" of all.

The Parent Pet Trap

*P*ets are such an obvious source of quality time and teaching moments with kids that it seems superfluous to write about all the benefits. From goldfish to gerbils, cats to canaries, and hamsters to horses, the menagerie of pet possibilities is endless. Every moment you spend teaching your kids how to care for animals is magnified many-fold by the larger life lessons you also teach: compassion, responsibility, selflessness, benevolence, humaneness. Pets can help kids grow their independence, and pets complete a triangle of companionship and love between you and your kids—each has a unique but interconnected relationship with the other.

Sounds idyllic, eh? But . . . I'm sure you can guess what I'm going to say next.

At the risk of sounding like the Grinch who stole Fido, here's a cautionary note: Remember that *No Regrets Parenting* is about finding quality time for special moments with your kids; it is not about spending time alone with "their" pets. Your days are hectic enough trying to fulfill adult responsibilities and salvage scarce minutes with your kids. Insofar as pets help you do the latter, terrific. But unless your kids are there with you to scrub the aquarium, change the litter box, fill the water bowl, clean the hutch, and throw the ball to the dog (even in a blizzard), I recommend you go to the zoo when your kids have a craving for a furry friend. If your kids aren't part of the triangle, pets become a parent trap. They take up precious time you could be spending more wisely with your kids. Ignore your kids' promises about taking full responsibility for the new pet they are pleading for; once the puppy settles in and the novelty wears off, they'll forget every vow they made. If your kids talk the talk, they have to walk the walk. And they have to walk the dog. Even in a blizzard.

The only way to protect yourself from the parent pet trap is with a contract. Contracts may seem a bit harsh when dealing with a five- or six-year-old, but they can be an important life lesson in and of themselves. A commitment is a commitment, and a contract formalizes a commitment. The contract needn't be written, although I prefer written agreements where pets are concerned—you can hang the contract on the cage or kennel and point to it whenever your kids forget whose pet it is and let the water bowl run dry. It can be as short as a line or two: "I promise that if Mommy and Daddy get a rabbit for me, I will feed and water my rabbit and help clean the hutch. If I don't, I know Mommy and Daddy may have to take my rabbit back to the animal shelter. Where it may get eaten by a Doberman." Okay, okay, you can leave out the last sentence. But you get the point.

You supervise, but the pet "belongs" to your child. The time you spend supervising is wonderful quality time—even the walks in the blizzard. But don't get caught out in the cold alone with your kids' pet.

Food

The Daily Dinner Meeting

*B*reakfast may be the "most important meal of the day," but dinner is the most important meal in the life of most families (see below[*] for an important disclaimer). At breakfast, everyone's in a rush to get where they have to be that day. Lunch? Fuggetaboutit. Nobody's home at the same time in the middle of the day. But dinnertime is the one recurring interlude in the day's disarray when the whole family may be able to coordinate their calendars and gather together. Everyone's hungry, everyone's pausing between the frenzy of the afternoon and the sometimes equally frenzied evenings, and everyone's tired and ready to sit down for a few minutes. When else do adults and kids have their biorhythms so synchronized?

By dinnertime, everyone in the household has accumulated a whole day's events to share with one another. There's good news and bad news, big developments and little developments. Every dinner is an opportunity to follow up on the discussions at dinner the night before. Look forward

---

[*]   Important disclaimer: As with all the suggestions in this book, remember that one size does not fit all. Every family is different and every strategy must be tailored to your own unique situation. In some households, for example, coordinating dinner schedules may be impossible: Dad works late most nights, Mom has dinner meetings, kids have early evening school activities, no one has time to slow down long enough to find each other for dinner. If that's your household, choose breakfast as your "must-meet meal." If everyone has an early morning, and even though everybody is rushed, make time for short breakfast meetings. Adjust the meeting "agenda" to the meal you choose: At breakfast, talk about the day before, or the day ahead, or plans for the weekend. Just be sure to talk.

That's the whole point of a meeting.

to dinner as a chance to reconnect with the people most important to you. Take turns telling the day's stories. As I dragged myself in the door after work, our kids would sometimes shout, "Wait till you hear what I have to say at dinner tonight!" What a wondrous thing to hear from a child.

It may start out slowly—come to dinner prepared with specific questions, because kids need prompting. When you ask, "So, what happened today?" they will typically answer "Nothing" or "Not much." "How was your day?" "Good." Don't settle for that. Prepare for your daily dinner meeting at home the way you prepare for your meetings at work— armed with an agenda of items you want to learn from your kids, and with news of your own day to share. Use what you talked about last night to start tonight's dinner conversation: "Did your English teacher give back your essay?" "Did your friends get in trouble for gluing the stapler to the desk?" "What did Enid decide about going to camp this summer?" "How did the tryouts go?" Show your kids that you remember what's going on in their lives and that you're interested. Here's a confession: I've even been known (only to myself, because I've never told this to anyone before) to make notes during the day about what I wanted to ask the kids at dinner, just to make sure I didn't forget and let a whole day go by without hearing the latest update. No, I didn't bring the notes to dinner . . . but I did secretly sneak a peek at them before going to the table.

Be there for dinner. Put it on your calendar (at least your mental calendar) every day: "dinner meeting with family." Even if you have to go back to work afterward, be there to share the day's events with your kids—theirs and yours. Insist that everyone be at dinner every night. You're allowed to make rules—you're the parent! Dinner together is one of the most important rules you'll ever make—and may be one of the hardest for you yourself to follow. But it's worth it. While you're making rules, make one more: no phone calls, text messages, or other interruptions during dinner (except emergencies, of course).

Soon you'll find yourself addicted to family dinners, and upset on the very rare nights that unavoidable conflicts arise.

After-School Snacks

As your kids get older, the closing bell at school simply signals the beginning of more time commitments and programmed activities. Playdates, clubs, and sports quickly fill the few hours between the end of school and dinner. Make no mistake, these are critically important activities for your kids' growth and for your sanity. For many parents, after-school hours are still the middle of the workday, and knowing that your kids are engaged in safe and healthy activities provides peace of mind and fulfills a practical necessity.

But when your kids are still young enough to have half-day preschool or to come straight home after school, and on the days, rare as they may be, that you can be there to welcome them, a golden window into their day opens for you. The kitchen table or the sofa in the family room becomes a debriefing center, complete with milk and cookies or fruit and crackers. When it's warm, sit on the porch, or pack snacks and stop at a park on the way home. This is downtime where you get the chance to hear about their day while their memories are still fresh on the subject. As with dinnertime (see the previous chapter), don't accept "good" as an answer to "How was your day?" or "nothing" to "What's new in school?" Ask the right questions so you get multi-word responses, and withhold the cookies until you do. Tell them about your day, too, so you can earn a cookie.

Moments for after-school snacks are often brief because real life comes calling—your work, their homework, errands, and dinner preparation. But brief is okay, because it's not long until dinner, when you will have the time you need to finish the conversations you started.

Tomorrow's Lunch Tonight

It's rare that families can eat lunch together—we're all too scattered during the day. That's why I stressed how important the daily dinner meeting is a couple chapters back. But there is a way to "share" lunch and to squeeze in a few more minutes together before bedtime. With homework done and pajamas on, gather the clan in the kitchen to make tomorrow's lunch. Rather than pulling together all the lunches by yourself, help each other fill the lunchboxes or sacks that everyone will grab in their rush out the door tomorrow morning. Not only does this make it more likely that the kids will like what they find in their lunches, but it also decompresses the morning flail just a bit. While you and your kids are pillaging the fridge and the pantry, teach them healthy food choices, listen (dance?) to a music CD they like, gossip a little, and talk about what's happening in their day tomorrow. While you're at it, nibble a bedtime snack or finish the dinner dishes together.

Then, after the kids have gone to bed, slip a little surprise into the lunchbox they just packed, like a note that says "I love you." Or maybe something a little unhealthy, like a chocolate kiss.

The Corner Diner

A friendly neighborhood restaurant can become a wonderful excuse for spending, and extending, special dinnertime moments with your kids. Kids are creatures of habit (as, for that matter, are grownups). Kids don't need variety or diversity in their eateries—they probably even order the same item off the menu each time they go to their favorite place. Just the announcement that "we're going to the Corner Diner" can awaken the tired and taciturn souls that your kids often become by dinnertime. Use the restaurant to celebrate special events or to perk up a difficult week. Walk to the restaurant if you're close enough (that's why I named it the Corner Diner!)—that gives you even more time to talk.

Your special family restaurant doesn't have to be fancy or expensive; in fact, the more casual and laid-back, the better. The less the food costs, the more often you can enjoy the place; the healthier the fare, the better you'll feel about taking your kids there. It's not the gourmet ambience that your kids get excited about when you go out to eat, it's the simple enjoyment of going someplace special. Favorite foods on the menu stimulate the "pleasure centers" and flip on the "fun buttons" in your kids' brains (see Part 1 of this book), which increases their focus and their participation in the event. Sharing time with your kids while their brains and bellies are happy and satisfied makes you a part of that happiness and satisfaction.

It may sound heretical, in this day of an obesity crisis, to link food with good feelings and good times. But happy times your kids spend with you at the Corner Diner will not make them fat. What makes them fat is sitting in front of the TV or computer for hours at a time without you, eating junk food.

What about takeout, the drive-through, and fast-food places? Each may have its place in your family dynamic, and the speed and convenience of those venues can be attractive and fun. But the extra time you spend sitting down together at the Corner Diner—waiting for the server to bring your order, for the water glasses to be refilled, and for the check to finally arrive—gives you moments with your kids that are lost at home to the pull of the TV, cell phones, video games, and the backyard. Kids are captives in a sit-down restaurant— nowhere to run, nowhere to hide. Intimate time, knees touching in the tiny booth, sharing the news of the day.

And for bringing all of you these cherished moments together, give your compliments to the chef.

Taco Night

*D*inner at home with the whole family is special unto itself, but there are easy ways to make it even more special. Taco night, pizza night, Chinese night, egg night, pancake night. You already know that kids love to go out to eat, and they're often more animated and engaged in a restaurant than they are at home (see the previous chapter). But you don't need to go to restaurants to have fun venues and exotic menus. Turn your kitchen into a Japanese sushi bar or an Italian bistro once a week—or do each on a different night for twice the weekly benefit. Your kids will be even more excited about sitting down together if they have their favorite foods on a regular basis. And when kids are excited and having fun, they are energized in their conversation and in sharing their news at the dinner table.

Special dinner nights are also unique opportunities to increase your kids' involvement in the meal making, and thereby increase the quality time you spend with them. When there are recurring themes for dinner, kids can assume bigger roles in getting the food to the table, because they'll start to remember the routine from the last taco night. Washing the vegetables, stacking the tortillas, mixing the salsa, grating the cheese, and gossiping about the latest news from school. You're still in charge of blending the margaritas! What a nice cantina you've created.

When the kids leave for school in the morning, remind them: "Taco night tonight!" They'll look forward to it all day.

Ice Cream Sundaes, Hot Cocoa, and Popcorn

*Y*es, there is an obesity crisis in this country, and we certainly don't want to teach our kids that food brings comfort or that eating means security—reinforcing the physical and psychological joys of food is not a healthy parenting strategy. But . . . kids have to be kids, and when kids grow up to become adults and parents (I'm talking about you!), they still need to occasionally feel like kids.

Establish special traditions around fun treats—they become more special because they don't happen often. Hot summer Sunday afternoon sundaes, or cold winter family TV nights with hot cocoa, or full-moon parties with moon-shaped cookies, or popcorn balls on days of the big game. Sprinkles make ice cream special, cuddling goes great with cocoa, black and white icing dresses up cookies, and popcorn is almost healthy for your kids. Now, please don't go around telling people that a pediatrician told you to feed your kids ice cream sundaes with sprinkles; I do have a professional reputation to maintain. So, for the official record, baked apples with cinnamon and raisins, angel food strawberry shortcake, snow cones made with apple juice, and banana splits with fat-free frozen yogurt work just as well and with less guilt.

The food is not the point—it just helps make the point. Fun foods and special treats are conversation starters and memory makers; they help imprint your kids' minds with images of the great moments you spend with them, and flip on the focus switches in their brains that you read about in Part 1. Your kids may not remember all the discussion topics or the jokes or the tickling, but they'll forever fondly recall the chocolate syrup and the marshmallows. Or baked apples and raisins ☺.

And, of course, they'll remember the occasions that merited the special treats. And that they shared them with you.

Food Fights

Just kidding. Bad idea. Move on to the next section.

Getting There

The Fly on the Dashboard

*Y*ou need to get to work and your kids need to get to school. Perfect. Every morning presents a new opportunity to spend a few bonus minutes together. Even if you're heading in opposite directions, arrange your daily start time so you can drive car pool. Many schools even have an earlier drop-off option for working parents. Yes, your kids are still half asleep, you are already girding yourself for the upcoming hassles at work, there are other kids in the car, and traffic is a nuisance.

But driving car pool tunes you in to each upcoming day in your kids' lives. Do they have gym today or study hall? Did they remember to bring their homework? Do they need a signed note for the field trip—and where is the field trip going, anyway? Is there a student assembly today? What's going on after school? Is that kid still being a nuisance at recess? What tests do they have today? Whoops! Better practice their spelling words on the way, too!

Car pool also lets you eavesdrop on real-time conversations between your kids and their friends. It is one of the well-known truisms of parenting that the driver of a car full of kids becomes invisible to the kids in the car—they act and talk and laugh and confide in each other as if the car was driving itself. Driving car pool is like being the proverbial "fly on the wall" during a few moments of your kids' social lives. It gives you a chance to hear how your kids relate to their friends, learn what kind of people your kids' friends really are, and get the scoop on what's important to your kids and their friends at these very random moments in their lives. What could be better than that?

Kids coming home from school are more animated (and more awake) than they are in morning car pool. If you can drive car pool home from school, you'll hear them talk about their day and about the homework they have to do that night (I can't count how many times I learned about a project assigned last week—and due tomorrow!— from the conversation in the backseat on the way home from school). You'll catch up on who said what to whom, and about who's going out with whom. And all of this occurs without the kids ever noticing that you're there—the invisible chauffeur.

H. G. Wells, roll over!

School Bus Magic

I f you don't have the privilege (☺; see the previous chapter) of driving car pool because your kids take the bus, spend a few minutes with them at the curb each morning before the bus gets there. These can be magical together moments, otherwise lost in the name of expediency, or drowned out by the cacophony of "music" blasting from your kids' MP3 earbuds.

The few minutes of your morning that you give up by waiting with your kids for the bus help you bring the day into focus, for both you and your kids. Ask them about what's going on at school today; tell them what you'll be doing at work; remind them about volleyball practice after school; quiz them on their geography for today's test; finish a conversation you started at the dinner table the night before; tease them about the special surprise dinner you have planned for tonight. When you add up all the bonus minutes you spend with your kids before the bus arrives, it amounts to more than fifteen hours each year if you're at the curb for just five minutes each school morning (thirty hours each year if the bus is running late!). That's time you'll never get back if you don't take advantage of it now.

And when the bus arrives, give them a big hug and tell them you can't wait to see them after school. Or, depending on their ages, sneak away before they have time to be mortified at the possibility of the other kids on the bus spotting you.

Road Trip

The best vacations are those that give you and your kids the most time together, without distractions and without interruptions. For any of you who have driven even short distances with young kids, this may seem like insane advice, but road trips can be the best family vacations of all. The time in the car, especially when your kids are "middle aged" (five to twelve), is priceless "captive audience" time.

Making the most of road trips takes some creativity and planning. Stop at weird roadside attractions, eat at funky diners along the way, have family debates, play highway games that everyone in the car can play together (license-plate poker, I Spy, mileage math, states and their capitals, Twenty Questions). Have contests to see who can sing the words to the most songs on the radio (tip: you'll have to find an oldies station to give yourself a chance in that competition).

Most Important Road Trip Rule: no devices allowed that isolate you or your kids from each other. This is tough, because MP3 players and cell phones can be so tightly attached to your kids' heads that you may have considered surgical removal. You'll undoubtedly have to learn to live with connectivity conflict again when you get back home—but on the road, when you've got the kids to yourselves, keep them to yourselves. No calling, texting, or videos on cell phones; no tiny white wires dangling from their ears.

When you make the road trip an adventure, the destination is even less important than the getting there and the getting back. Compare that with flying to a crowded theme park when there's little chance for everyone to talk to each other on the airplane (though I suppose the long security lines at the airport could be viewed as "together time"), and when you get there, the theme park *attractions* are really *distractions* from the time you can spend with the kids. Or compare a road trip to flying with the "family-friendly resort" when again there's no face time on the airplane, and the resort is loaded with "kids' activities" that separate you from them for most of the trip. I know, I know, kids-only activities sound like a great idea—you'd like a little adult time on vacation, too. Understandable. So if you're going to a theme park or family-friendly resort, at the very minimum make sure everyone sits down to dinner together every night, and try to schedule at least some daytime activities that you all can do together. If you have enough vacation days, drive to the resort or theme park to lessen the impact of the distractions and separation once you arrive. That way, by the time you get there, you've already had real family time together, and on the drive home, you get a chance for a real family recap.

If the biggest benefit of road trips is the up close and personal time in the car, van, or RV, the next biggest benefit of a driving vacation is the lower cost compared with flying. Remember my promise in the "Money" chapter in Part 1 that the best times with your kids can be those that are free or inexpensive. Money for vacations is almost always tight, and even long road trips can be pricey when you factor in gas, motels, and food along the way—but they rarely add up to airfare. There are ways of cutting road trip costs, as well: Camp out, pack food from home, and visit state parks and attractions that are closer and cheaper to get to. Your kids will remember vacations by how much fun they have, not by how exotic or expensive the trip.

Vacation Bribery

When your kids are young, they go where you go for vacation. That's a real blessing, because as they get older, it's harder and harder to interest your kids in family vacations. They may already be in college or have summer jobs, busy social lives, and even invitations to join their friends on vacations. This is where you need to be especially creative. If you can afford "exotic" trips—Hawaii, Alaska, the Caribbean, Europe—that's great; even the busiest older kids, and the ones usually too cool to want a vacation with Mom and Dad, will bite on the exotic temptation. But for most of us, the extravagant vacation bribe is a rare or impossible luxury, so we need to tone down the bait without decreasing its effectiveness in getting the older kids onboard.

Tailor the vacation to your kids' passions. Are they baseball fanatics? Drive to spring training in Arizona or Florida, and buy the cheap seats on the outfield grass. Football? Go to their favorite team's August training camp, where you can watch practices for free. Addicted to a special TV show? Write for free tickets to sit in the studio audience and plan your trip around the show. Movie lovers? Tour one of the big film studios. Chocoholics or candy addicts? The Hershey factory in Pennsylvania, or the Jelly Belly factory in California; dozens of other confectioners are only a short drive from wherever you live. There are factory tours to suit every interest and in virtually every locale. Crayon, soft drink, automobile, motorcycle, greeting card, computer, RV, and cheese factories are scattered all over the country, and almost all offer tours. Plan your trip around a dog show, music festival, horse race, NASCAR event, outdoor art show, or hot-air balloon festival. Tour Elvis's home or Opryland or the CNN studios. Museums usually make kids yawn, but some museums are cool—science fiction, rock music, comic books, computers, outer space, race cars, trains, ships, movies, and spies all have their own museums. There are also Hall of Fame museums for almost every taste in sports and culture. Tourist traps work because they exploit people's passions and satisfy their curiosities. Passion and curiosity are the same traits you should exploit in getting your kids excited about the family vacation.

Do you love camping and hiking but your kids are bored outdoors? Dial up the excitement factor with a canoe or kayak trip, rock climbing, spelunking, ice fishing, paintball, cross-country skiing, hut tripping, horseback riding, paragliding, or windsurfing. Make sure you factor in the cost of lessons so you don't have to factor in the cost of emergency medical care.

Let your kids help plan the trip, and let them tell you what would make it more special for them. They may want to bring a friend—it's better to have your kids' friends on your vacation than to have your kids desert you for their friends' vacations. (Prepare yourself for the day your kids ask to bring a boyfriend or girlfriend along. I'll leave it to you to handle that one, except to confide that we said yes.)

Admit it. Bribery is a big part of parenting at all ages, anyway. Why shouldn't it be a part of family vacation planning when your kids are old enough to have vacation ideas of their own?

Unplugged

*N*ext time you're at a stoplight, take a peek inside the minivan stopped next to you. The driver (parent) is talking on the phone; the kids (they're the ones with the white earbuds) are listening to "music" or watching the dropdown TV screen in the backseat, or texting on their own cell phones; and the family dog is staring at you through the partially open back window, desperate for someone to notice him. Only the dog is unplugged and fully aware of his surroundings. Each human is entranced in a personal digital space, separated from one another not by physical distance but by bandwidth.

Here's a radical idea based on my Most Important Road Trip Rule from a couple chapters back. Whenever you are en route in the car anywhere with your kids—be it for vacation, car pool, a dentist appointment, or to Grandma's house—allow no cell phones, Internet, MP3 players, TVs, or radios unless everyone in the car is sharing the same entertainment. That is, no personal digital, video, audio, or other electronic distractions permitted, for you or your kids, while traveling together by car. It's okay to listen to music or the ballgame together; the key word is *together*. And it's still okay to bring the dog.

Without the isolating gadgets, you'll have to resort to talking to each other. And teasing and laughing together. Is it okay for the kids to watch a movie together in the backseat while you're driving? Not for my money. How many captive moments with your kids can you afford to lose? Looking back someday, wouldn't you rather have been talking or singing or playing a word game?

For vacations, the beauty of camping or beach trips is that the connections to the outside world often fail at remote locations, so you don't have to be the bad guy who says "turn that off." You and your kids can concentrate on the setting and scenery, and enjoy the family bond and spirit that spending intimate time together creates, without digital interruptions. Now, imagine the possibilities of no Facebook, Twitter, e-mail, videos, text messaging, or iPods even for the more mundane travel required for running errands or commuting to after-school activities. Those trips are short enough that your kids will learn to do without the digital crutches of perpetual connectivity. Face time trumps Facebook, even if it's only a short reprieve.

There's also a potentially life-saving benefit to unplugging in the car. Talking and texting on cell phones while driving causes fatal traffic accidents, second in importance only to driving under the influence. You may think that it's okay for you to talk and drive because you are a much too careful and experienced driver to be easily distracted while driving. But even if you think of yourself as talented enough to juggle the phone, steer the wheel, put on the brakes, check the side and rearview mirrors, and monitor the traffic flow while talking or texting, is that the kind of behavior you want your kids to mimic someday when they drive? Remember, they are watching you. When you teach them that the car is an unplugged zone, you'll capture precious moments with them that otherwise would have been lost to digital distractions. And unplugging will become a habit, just like putting on a seat belt, which will make them safer someday soon when they get behind the wheel themselves.

By the time your kids get home from their unplugged travel, they will undoubtedly be going through withdrawal. Recognize that they need to reestablish their networks, and give them some unstructured time, space, and privacy to log back on.

You probably need to check your messages, too.

Sleepaway Camp Runamok

Important disclaimer: For those of you lifelong summer sleepaway camp families, please skip this chapter, or be forewarned and forgive me in advance for what I'm about to tell you. My goal in writing this book is to give you new ideas and new approaches to finding time with your kids, not to disrupt family traditions that work well for you. You needn't fix what's not broken. But, that said . . .

I am not a fan of sleepaway camps. Soon enough your kids will move out—to college or to life's other endeavors that take them from you and your home. Why send them away prematurely? Sleepaway camp is like short-term boarding school. It is true that camp is a great experience for kids. It teaches them independence, self-reliance, interpersonal and social skills, and how to squat over a toilet seat to avoid physically touching anything in those disgusting bathrooms. And the friendships at sleepaway camp are intense and often lifelong. But kids can get almost all of those same benefits at day camp, and still come home for dinner every night, where they can share the experiences of their day with you, and vice versa. Kids can eat camp food, sing camp songs, play camp pranks—and still be home for a bedtime story and kiss goodnight.

Summers are important times in your family's life. Yes, you still have to work, and the kids still need to be happily occupied during the day. But without the burden of homework and the rigor of other school rituals, summers give your family leisurely evenings to linger over dinner on the patio, a ballgame at the stadium, the short walk or drive for ice cream, or a pajama walk through the neighborhood.

Day camps might be the best of all worlds for your family: structured time during the day when you're busy with work, and evenings spent together doing the things you never take the time for during the school year. And you'll be able to afford more evening activities with all the money you'll save by not paying room and board at sleepaway camp. Why give up summer evenings with your kids by sending them away from home before you have to?

Walk, Don't Run (and Don't Drive)

If someone did a study (someone probably has) on the average distance we drive with each outing, we'd surprise ourselves at how often we drive our kids short distances to "save time" and "increase efficiency." Indeed, driving can and does often save time and increase efficiency, but at what cost? The minutes we "save" by driving our kids to soccer practice at the neighborhood park are actually priceless and irreplaceable moments with them that we lose in the name of convenience.

Next time you need to take your kids somewhere nearby, walk. Walking with your kids is a great way to slow down the pace of your lives and have more unscripted moments with them. As you remember from Part 1, the "mosey button" in their brains focuses kids' attention on their time with you and on what you hope to impart to them when you're together.

Clearly, walking where you have to go is not always possible—you may have to go too far and/or need to be there too quickly. But whenever time and distance allow, walk. And while you're walking, talk—about where you're going, what you're thinking, what they're thinking, what you see on the way, what's for dinner, who said what to whom in school today. Talk about small things or big things or medium-size things. Hold hands with your kids while you're walking if they haven't gotten too cool for that yet; if they have, put your arm around their shoulder occasionally to punctuate your conversation (and then remove your arm before any of their friends in the neighborhood see!).

The beauty of walking is that even though you may have to plan where you're going, you don't have to plan the getting there—what happens along the way is spontaneous. If you're dropping your kids off somewhere (a playdate, piano lessons, karate) and you would normally drive away only to return later for a pick-up, bring along a backpack with work or reading and find a quiet place to wait until your kids are finished. The hour or two that you have alone, in a coffee shop or under a shade tree, helps you slow down, stay sane, and distance yourself a little from the pressures that would otherwise find you if you drove straight home or to work.

Then pick up your child and walk home together!

Driver's Ed

There are important "attention buttons" that I described in Part 1 of this book that lock your kids into what they are doing and to what you are telling them; when you trigger these buttons, it helps them appreciate the special moments they spend with you. The "fun button" is among the most effective—that's the one that helps them better remember your lesson about looking both ways before crossing the street when the street you're crossing happens to lead to the ice cream store.

Adolescence can be a trying time. Kids pull back from parents and may become too cool or too busy for the usual family togetherness activities. That's normal—the teen years are a period of staggering biological and emotional changes for kids. Separation is to be expected—and is absolutely necessary to get them ready for THE moment when they leave for college. But there is a simple secret for you to again become their first choice of people with whom to "hang." You haven't been this cool in their eyes since, well, those walks across the street to the ice cream store.

The simple secret? Teach your kids to drive. If leaving for college is THE moment (and it is), driving alone for the first time is THE mini-moment. The independence that driving brings for a child is essential preparation for the even greater independence that college brings. Just as you should be a major part of preparing your child for THE moment when you leave her for the first time in her new dorm room, you should be a major part of preparing her for THE mini-moment when she pulls out of the driveway for the first time on her own.

Not since crossing the street for tutti-frutti with sprinkles on top has your child been so excited about learning from you. Back in the day, all kids learned to drive from their parents. While many still do, driving schools have taken over the primary teaching role for families that can afford the cost and/or can't bear the stress. But even if you hire out your kids' primary driver's education to a school, you should take every chance you have to drive with them. The car key is also the key to make them want to spend every minute they can with you between the ages of fifteen and sixteen. Don't believe me? Try these magical words and see what happens: "Hey, I'm running an errand. Wanna drive?" The bedroom door flies open, the MP3 earbuds come off their heads, and they log off Facebook, all in the time it takes you to find your wallet.

And now you've got them right where you want them. You've pushed their attention button. They are just excited enough, and hopefully just fearful enough, to listen with rapt attention to what you tell them. Sure, you need to remind them of proper braking distance, centering the car in the lane, and avoiding the blind spot by looking over their shoulder when changing lanes. But don't miss the bigger opportunity. You have a captive audience—the last time they were so willingly trapped with you in the car was when they were buckled into their car seats eating Cheerios. At the stop lights, find out about school and ask about their friends. When you get to wherever your errand takes you, have them join you in the store, or at the mechanic's garage, or in the post office to continue your conversation. When you get back in the car, shift back into driver's ed mode—remind them that parking lots can be as dangerous as streets and to always watch for little kids dashing out from between the cars.

For old time's sake, before you head home, have your new driver take you to the ice cream store for tutti-frutti with sprinkles. Use the drive-through—remind him to look both ways before turning in! You've pushed his "fun button," and he's listening to every word you say.

Entertainment

FAMILY MOVIE NIGHT

Take this as the cultural challenge of our times—finding movies that are appropriate and enjoyable for everyone in the family. Like taco night and minor holidays, family movie nights can be little big events—times with the kids that take little planning, little money, and little energy while producing big memories. Going out to the movies is fun but can be expensive. There are so many alternatives, from renting a DVD to "on demand" movies at home, that the only trick left to seeing movies as a family is picking the right one. And even picking the right movie becomes another chance to spend precious moments with your kids. Instead of screening all the movies yourself, involve your kids in the process of picking age-appropriate films that appeal to the genre preferences of all of the kids. Some nights the action fans may have to watch "chick flicks," and vice versa—but never compromise on the idea that everyone watches together. This is also a chance to force a little culture on your kids—occasionally, make them watch a "classic," because no child should ever leave for college without having seen *Casablanca, Butch Cassidy and the Sundance Kid,* and *Dr. Zhivago.*

If you're watching at home, enforce the movie theater rule—no cell phones allowed. Make sure you pop the popcorn and fetch the snacks before the movie starts to mimic the theatergoing fun. And then, most important, after it's over, whether you've been in the theater or at home, conduct a formal review process, where each child turns movie critic. Everyone has to "score" the movie on a 1 to 10 scale, or grade it, A through F, and give reasons for their rating. The idea is not to debate which score is right or wrong, but rather to teach your kids to give, and let you receive, honest feedback on their tastes and preferences. Don't give your own rankings, because if your score is closer to one of your kids' ratings than to another, it will look like you're taking sides or that there is a "right" answer. Scoring a movie teaches your kids to formulate and express their opinions without embarrassment or fear of "being wrong." Rotate the order of asking your kids for their ranking—but start with the youngest more often, lest he always pick the same score as his older sibs. Scoring is your chance to see what tickles their funny bones, or scares the daylights out of them, or makes them think. It's also a guide for you in choosing future family movie night entertainment. But best of all, it's another excuse to share time with your kids even after the credits roll.

The real motive for seeing movies as a family, of course, is that your kids are the only ones who can figure out how to work the DVD player and the remote.

TV Guide

*B*ecause there are so many better activities to share with kids, you probably assumed that TV wouldn't make it into this book. Well, let's get real. TV is a big part of our kids' culture. Even if you restrict TV time in your home, your kids will find it at their friends' homes or, even worse, feel like outcasts when their friends talk about the hot shows. Much as with family movie nights, TV can be our friend, and another avenue to quality time spent together. Pick your favorite family TV shows. Make sure your choices are age appropriate for your kids and, ideally, suitable for everyone to watch together. When your kids are young, the shows may be animated or on the kids' channels. As your kids get older, more sophisticated fare is in order. You don't all have to be available when the show runs— record it and watch together when you can synchronize an hour of downtime. Unlike family movie night, you don't need a big chunk of time to catch up with this week's thirty-minute or one-hour episode. Use the TV as an occasional before-bedtime treat, or a perfect snowy weekend day warm-up activity after shoveling the walks.

And then, like you do with family movie nights and most other activities in this book, talk about the show together. Knowing what's on TV, I can guarantee that the discussion will almost always be better than the show.

Family University

TV game and quiz shows have permeated our society so thoroughly that it seems like we ought to get something redeeming back in exchange for all the flashing lights, clanging bells, and celebrity blather our kids are exposed to. Enter Family University. Rather than everyone zoning out while watching TV's spinning wheels and deals (or no deals), design and play your own "quiz show" that's tailored to perfectly fit your kids' knowledge and interest levels. Play Family University after dinner, on weekends, before bedtime, and especially during summers when your kids' brain activity is at its nadir. Your kids are the contestants.

It's easy to find quiz questions for kids—use their school books; check out subject review books from the library; or go online to find sample questions from all the standardized tests your kids have to take. But don't limit yourself to school subjects—make it more fun by mixing in questions about movie and music stars, cartoon characters, your kids' favorite storybooks, TV shows, and anything else that captures their fancy. You can get lots of ideas, and already-written questions at age-appropriate levels, on the games shelf at the toy store. Look for trivia and brain teaser games, flash card sets, and home versions of those TV quiz shows we're avoiding.

The point is not to sterilize your kids' fun or immunize them against popular media and culture (see the previous two chapters)—the point is to take them away from the TV and put them right in front of you, laughing and learning.

High School Musical
(and High School Football)

The best family entertainment buys of today are brought to you by your neighborhood high school. For a few bucks, and often for free, you can take your kids to see classic Broadway shows; varsity sports; holiday concerts; competitions in geography, math, speech, and engineering; and debates and cooking contests. High school events provide a wholesome opportunity for parents of pre–high school kids to take advantage of the natural idolizing that young kids have for older kids. For a seven-year-old baseball fan, the local high school baseball team is perfect entertainment—and most schools even sell hot dogs. Does your daughter love *High School Musical*? Take her to the next high school musical! Is your middle schooler a math and science whiz? Take her to the next bridge-building or egg-drop contest at the high school. Most high schools now have Web sites (does anyone not have a Web site?) where you can check for upcoming events.

The best part for parents comes afterward, when you and your kids can discuss your favorite scene in the school play, the razzle-dazzle quarterback option play, the merits of each side of the debate, or the coolest bridge design. It's during these post-event moments that your kids and you get an early insight into what their future high school interests might be.

Alas, what if your kids are already in high school and they attend their school events with friends rather than with you? Take them to local college events! Even the coolest high school basketball player or cheerleader will want to see what's next—how does college basketball or cheerleading compare with high school? Take your high schooler to the college game (or musical) this weekend, and buy him a soft pretzel to chew on while you discuss . . . your favorite scene in the play, the razzle-dazzle quarterback option play, the merits of each side of the debate, or the coolest bridge design. And yes, it's during these post-event moments that your high schoolers and you get an early insight into what their future college and career interests might be.

THE LIBRARY (OR BOOKSTORE)

Teach your kids to love libraries. These are wonderful places with unlimited opportunities for sharing, browsing, sitting on laps, reading stories, and learning the value of free entertainment. A library card should be the first thing you put in your child's first wallet or purse. Find your favorite spot in the library, and go there often. When your kids are younger, their favorite spot is likely in the kids' section. As they get older, it may be in the cushy chairs next to the new-fiction shelves. Sometimes you may want to take your work and their homework to the library if everyone needs a change of venue for the daily routines.

Libraries come in branches, close to home. But the best part about libraries is that the reading selection is different than in your home. The second best part is that the books are free—find the ones they love, check them out, read them over and over again together for a couple weeks, and then swap them for a new set.

Bookstores can serve similar purposes of together time with special spots for reading—the small independents have little reading nooks, but even the big-box stores have plenty of cushy chairs scattered about. Some of the stores even have your favorite gourmet coffee nearby. Of course, the bookstore books aren't free, but once you find the ones your kids love, remember the titles for birthday and holiday gifts, or go to the library and check them out.

However you choose to use your time in the library or bookstore, the outcome is always good: it's time with your kids, reinforcing the joys of reading, and serving up plenty of lively discussion and idea-sharing—and more insight into how your kids think about things. All this, and no admission fee required.

Play

Personal Trainer and Coach

Teach your kids to play sports. It's fair to assume, I think, that most of you are not professional athletes. But there is a magical stage in your kids' growth and development when you are better at sports than they are. Warning: That stage doesn't last very long for most of us, so you should take advantage of it while it lasts. The beauty of teaching sports to kids is that it is an intimate, healthy, and fun interaction that requires no set time, no special location, and no expense other than the cost of a volleyball, baseball mitt, or tennis racket. Even if you haven't bounced a ball since your own childhood, you start out being better than your kids at just about any sport. Try several sports and see which of them your kids (and you) enjoy the most. Kick the ball around when you get home from work; throw a softball while waiting for the school bus with your kids in the morning; shoot a few hoops at the park on weekends.

Before you know it, your kids may show a talent for one of the sports you've tried with them—or they may have no talent at all, but just enjoy playing the game. That's the time to transition to an organized neighborhood program that can teach kids more than you can about the sport, and let them socialize with other kids who are making the same transition. Encourage your kids to play hard, and teach them what it means to be a good sport. Use sports as a teaching tool for life lessons. Winning and losing. Self-improvement. Trying your best. Being part of a team. Overcoming disappointment. Dealing with people who can be difficult.

When your kids start neighborhood or school sports, it doesn't mean your job is done. Get to your kids' games when you can, continue playing and practicing the sport with your kids, and warm up with them in the backyard or at the park before driving them to their games—at least until they start throwing the ball so hard you might get hurt! If you have the time, help coach the team; coaching is a wonderful example of the "subliminal togetherness" strategy I described in Part 1 of this book. Your child is part of a team, interacting with friends, oblivious to the fact that her parent is there with her—in her eyes, you're the coach, but your eyes still get to see your little star in action.

It's also important to know when your kids should stop neighborhood or school sports. The rule for stopping is simple: Stop when it's no longer fun for them. As kids get older, the competitiveness and intensity of sports may get to be too much, but your kids may be hesitant to tell you if they think you want them to keep playing. *No Regrets Parenting* is about really knowing your kids. This is no exception—be with them enough to know what they're enjoying and what they're not enjoying.

Other Pastimes

I don't like the word "pastimes" because it sounds as if the goal of these activities is to pass time, which seems so wasteful when time with your kids is so fleeting and precious. The goals of *No Regrets Parenting* are to maximize and optimize time lest it pass too quickly! Having said that, participating in pastimes with your kids can be very meaningful if you don't take the word literally. Think of pastimes as "share times" with your kids.

If your kids don't take to sports (see the previous chapter), fear not. Many relationships between parents and kids turn out just fine even without the bleacher blisters and sideline screaming that come with sports as your kids grow older and the competition heats up. Help your kids find other interests that you can be a part of, too—theater, scouting, dance, writing, art, music. These are a little harder for you to coach if you're not an actor, Eagle Scout, dancer, writer, artist, or musician yourself. Unlike sports, you may never be better than your kids at these pastimes, and getting your kids started can be a little less spontaneous and requires a little more planning. But that doesn't mean you can't get them started. Encourage your kids to try out for neighborhood and school theater productions and concerts. Start a family blog and have your kids write their own posts. Many schools offer after-school enrichment programs for nominal cost: dance, karate, drawing, science, etc. Then, when you and your kids are home together, have them show you what they've learned; let your kids be your teachers for these activities; practice with them.

A cautionary note is in order regarding pastimes, lest you become a "potpourri parent." That's the term I used in Part 1 of this book to describe the syndrome of über-parenting that relentlessly thrusts kids into a highly programmed "if-it's-Tuesday-it-must-be-violin-lessons-because-figure-skating-is-not-till-Wednesday" schedule. Potpourri parents subject their kids to constant activity in the hope that their kids will discover their innermost passion; the never-ending search for an experiential epiphany. Kids' of potpourri parents are far too busy for parents to meaningfully share the activities with them. That should not be the goal of pastimes.

As with everything else in *No Regrets Parenting*, sharing pastimes with your kids requires balance, along with your observational skills and intuition. When you are attuned to your kids' reactions, and there with your kids often enough to see those reactions, you'll learn what your kids enjoy, what they're good at, and what gives them a sense of accomplishment. Along the way, since you're sharing the pastime with your kids, you may even learn to sing or dance a little yourself.

Hobby Sharing

If you have a hobby, share it with your kids. If you don't have a hobby, kids are a great excuse to develop one. Hobbies can be the ultimate playdate, and another activity for you to "double dip," doing things with your kids that you all enjoy equally. When they are young, your kids will enjoy whatever hobby you enjoy. If you think it's cool, they'll think it's cool, and they'll love being part of your playtime. By the time they get a little older, even if your stamp or coin collection becomes passé for them, you've still had meaningful time together, and they have a deeper appreciation for what makes you tick. Especially if your hobby is fixing antique clocks. Sorry ☺.

While philately and numismatics may or may not capture your older kids' fancy, many adult hobbies are very cool even for the coolest kids. Radio-controlled cars (or boats and planes), fantasy football, jewelry design, fishing, computer geek stuff, cake design, moviemaking, electric trains, all-terrain vehicles, pottery, magic, sailing, origami, gourmet cooking, beadwork, baseball card collecting, photography . . . the list of cool hobbies goes on and on. If you're picking a new hobby to grow into with your kids, there are several factors to consider in your choice. First, your new hobby should be fun and stimulating for you so you'll stick with it; if you give up on your hobby, or flit from one fad to another, your kids will lose interest and you'll send them the wrong message about following through on projects and commitments. Second, make sure the new hobby is safe for them to continue on their own when they're a little older; your schedules won't always synchronize, and if you are lucky and pick a hobby that your kids really love, they will want to do it on their own when you're busy, or share it with their friends. For that reason, welding, electrical repair, taxidermy, and meat smoking might not be the best choices. Third, pick a conveniently located and easily accessible hobby. One of the best benefits of sharing a new hobby with your kids is that it helps you make the most of your time with them whenever that time pops up. Calendars and advance scheduling are very important for sharing planned moments with your kids, but occasionally surprises occur—soccer practice is rained out, your business meeting is postponed, or their school declares a snow day. If your hobby requires a long drive to the lake, the rock-climbing hill, or the skeet-shooting range, you probably won't make the effort with short notice or a brief window of time. But if everything you need is in the garage, the kitchen, the family room, or just a short drive away, you and your kids can have fun spontaneously, as soon as the opportunity occurs. Finally, pick a hobby that's cool enough that your kids may even choose to do it with you over the option of watching TV or playing video games alone in their rooms. Which brings up the obvious question: What about picking video games as your hobby to share with kids? For more on that, see the next chapter.

Now that you've involved your kids in your hobby or picked a new hobby to master together, you have to promise not to sneak off too often to play alone while they're in school!

Video Games—When in Rome

I am not a fan of video games for kids. I've read all the arguments in favor of them, trying to be responsive and fair to my kids' pleadings. But I'm unconvinced that the hand-eye coordination and tech savvy supposedly gained by these games can't be better gained with other activities (although I have to admit, I think I remember my mother telling me the same thing about my childhood addiction to pinball machines). That said, our family boycott of XBox, PlayStation, and Wii products didn't work out so well. Every other kid in the neighborhood, and in every other neighborhood, has these diabolical digital devices. Video games are hooked up to TV screens, computer screens, and phones. They can be handheld and easily concealed in classrooms and under the dinner table. Video games are inescapable. But our video game–less home was not inescapable—our kids simply escaped to their friends' houses, where they spent playdate hours making up for lost time. So . . . when in Rome, you may have to do as the Romans do, lest all the Romans defect to Greece, if you know what I mean.

If you do decide to cave in and bring the magic of video games into your home, at least do your best to screen the games and, gasp, maybe even learn them so you can experience this part of your kids' free time with them, too. Does playing video games with your kids qualify as quality time? Setting personal bias aside, I have to say that I think playing video games with your kids probably does qualify. First, your kids will "kick your butt," to use their phrasing; this is one activity where you'll never have to let them win, and it's a good thing for kids to occasionally see their parents as human and vincible. Second, there will be guaranteed hilarity at your lack of dexterity; your lack of prosperity (these items are not cheap) won't be as funny. Finally, some games have somewhat redeeming virtual reality, because they closely mimic real-world activities such as table tennis, bowling, baseball, skiing, and dancing (which are much better, in my mind, than games where you blow each other up). Of course, those video games that mimic real-world activities beg the question of why not just do the real versions of table tennis, bowling, baseball, skiing, and dancing. But there's my bias again.

Bottom line: if video games are important to your kids and you can afford to indulge them, suck it up and try to see the games as just another route for getting closer to your kids and their world.

And set time limits, lest their virtual realities take over their reality.

Toy Story and Game Theory

If you're able to avoid the video game lure, and even if you succumb to it, your choices of non-digital games and toys for your kids are plentiful—kids are a big, big market. Choose carefully. There are several goals to strive for in picking playthings for your kids. First, they should be affordable; second, they should lend themselves to play both with and without you. That is, you want to pick toys and games you can play with your kids, and that kids can play on their own when you're busy. Finally, the items you pick for your kids should encourage communication and interaction—solitary play is okay once in awhile and helps build independence, but group play is more than play, it's socialization. And when you're part of the group playing, it's quality time with your kids.

Board games are fabulous for kids, and for your relationship with your kids, regardless of their ages. From Candy Land and Monopoly, to checkers and chess, to Scrabble and The Settlers of Catan, playing board games with your kids gives you access and insight into their thought processes and imaginations. Watch them scheme and strategize, see their competitive streaks gently peek out, and teach them the lessons of graceful losing and humble winning. Card games have many of the same advantages as board games and are even less expensive. You don't need pricey (and often presumptuous) "educational toys" to teach your kids the valuable lessons learned by interacting with others, nor should you feel that play always needs to be enlightening. Fun can just be fun, and playing with you is always fun for your kids.

Simple dolls and toy trucks can lead to creative play and storytelling with your kids. Perhaps the best toys of all are the "character" toys crafted from popular TV shows like *Sesame Street*, or from Disney movies and Spider-Man. These hard rubber statuettes (or, if your kids prefer, soft stuffed characters) encourage your kids to mimic the characters' voices and dialogue in made-up scenarios and homegrown scripts. Every evening's story line can be different. Your kids can play among themselves or with friends, but whenever you can join the performance, jump right in. You'll usually be assigned to play the "bad guy" to your kids' superheroes, but don't you often feel like that's your role in the family anyway?!!

Outdoors

Just a Walk in the Park (or Zoo)

*Y*our tax dollars are nowhere better spent than on the creation and maintenance of public parks and zoos. Whether you have your own big backyard or live on the fifteenth floor of a high-rise, parks provide special moments with your kids that other settings can't match for the price (free!). Well, yes, there are the taxes, but you have to pay those whether you take advantage of the parks or not, so you might as well take advantage.

Picnics; soccer matches or softball games for playing or watching; baseball fields; basketball and tennis courts; climbing towers with slides; monkey bars; and swing sets. And each piece of equipment, playing field, stretch of grass, or walking trail provides new opportunities for chatter, laughter, and memory-making with your kids. Which park was it where you taught your daughter to swing a tennis racket, and how many times were you able to ping the ball back and forth during that first lesson? On which hoop did you teach your son to make a lay-up? Which was the best sledding hill? The perfect picnic spot? Isn't that the tree our kite got stuck in? Remember feeding the ducks on the pond? Or how we collected the prettiest leaves during fall?

If you are close enough, walk or bike to the park to extend the serenity of the day. Parks are also a great place for applying the "subliminal togetherness" strategy with your kids as described in Part 1 of this book. Depending on their age, you can turn them loose to play on their own, socialize with other kids, explore their environment, play sports—all with you hovering just far enough away that they can develop their independence without noticing your watchful presence. Bring a book and find a shade tree where you have a great view of their growth and maturation.

Is there any place as fun for young kids as the zoo? The time you spend strolling past the animals, pointing fingers, and laughing at the silly-looking Malayan tapir or the scary Abyssinian hornbill is pure and wholesome entertainment of the non–video game, non-TV type. Have everyone pick their favorite reptiles or choose names for the monkeys (your kids may *not* use their siblings' names in this game!). All of the same togetherness benefits of the zoo can be found at the aquarium, if your town has one. When your kids are a little older, the botanical gardens may catch their fancy, although funny ferns are not nearly as captivating as furry friends for most kids.

Hooked at the Hip

In Part 1 of this book I describe "double dipping" as a strategy for spending more quality time with your kids while still taking care of yourself and staying sane. The "double dip" approach is to find activities that you and your kids would enjoy doing without each other and then do them together. There are lots of examples throughout the book. But outdoor activity and exercise offer the most options for "double dipping." Why? Because so many of the most popular and healthy forms of exercise can be tailored to your fitness goals *and* to your kids' ability levels.

BIKING—You can't beat bikes for inexpensive and healthy double dipping. Devices now exist to take kids of almost any age along for the ride—from trailers to trailer cycles, "pre-bikes," and tandem bikes. And, of course, when the kids are big enough, they get their own set of wheels to ride alongside you. Explore different trails to keep it interesting for you and an adventure for your kids. When the kids are old enough to read a map, plan the route together; when they're still hooked up to your bike in a trailer, talk to them as you're riding and tell them where you're riding. Teach them trail etiquette and turn signals. Play I Spy, or the "hold your breath, here comes a bump" game, or count how many animals they can spot along the way. Exercise, fresh air, and fresh scenery.

SWIMMING—When your kids are little, they need full-time supervision in the pool, so bring an adult buddy who also has kids, and tag team—you swim laps while your buddy makes sure all the water wings are in place, and then he swims while you're on pool-noodle duty. As your kids get older, they can play with friends while you exercise in the pool. If adult lap hours are different than open swim hours, start a personal water aerobics program for yourself to keep moving while your kids swim; then when lap time begins, sit them down with a healthy snack on the pool chairs.

JOGGING/WALKING—Like bike trailers, jogging strollers let you bring even the littlest ones along for the run. Or let your "middle-age" kids bike alongside as you jog. If you have a dog, this becomes "triple dipping"!

KARATE LESSONS—If you and your kids are beginners, find a martial-arts sensei (teacher) who will let you take lessons together. But when you reach the level at which you are paired off for fighting matches, it's probably a good idea to ask for an unrelated opponent.

SNOWSHOEING—Skiing and snowboarding are great if you live near the mountains and can afford the lift tickets. But the youngest kids aren't allowed on the slopes, and toddlers and "middle-age" kids are usually relegated to the bunny slopes, far from where you'd like to be skiing. Much less expensive than skiing, though, and without the requirement of a mountain, snowshoeing is invigorating winter exercise for almost all ages. As the slogan goes, anyone who can walk can snowshoe. And for your prewalkers and toddlers who tire quickly, put them in a sled hooked up to a waist leash and pull them behind you.

HIKING—This one is actually easiest when your kids are little and can fit in a Snugli or backpack child carrier. The whining doesn't usually start until your kids are old enough to walk, but would much prefer walking in the mall; for a solution to this problem, see the next chapter and the "Vacation Bribery" chapter.

ROWING—For kids younger than teens, it's best to keep canoe, kayak, and rowboat outings limited to gentle lakes and streams rather than raging rivers. But the aerobic and upper-body workout for you is still fantastic. Kids of all ages love getting out on the water enough to happily put on their life jackets.

FISHING—Casting flies into a pristine lake or mountain river with your kids offers a whole new angle to the term "double dipping." The moments and memories you snag will be much more meaningful for all of you than anything that ends up on your line.

ROLLERBLADING AND ROCK CLIMBING—Some adult outdoor fitness activities can be a little tricky with kids of certain ages. These two are clearly not options for including infants the way you can with biking and jogging, and it's hard to safely skate or climb alongside young kids who are just learning. Some "double dipping" may prove to be "double slipping (and falling)" for many families, but may work well for yours.

You already know how great you feel after exercising outdoors; as further proof, a recent study from Britain found significant mental and physical health advantages of outdoor workouts compared with those in the gym.* And that study didn't even mention the "parental

---

* *Environmental Science & Technology* 45, No. 5 (2011): 1761–1772.

mental" health benefits of knowing that you have captured precious, and sweaty, moments with your kids.

Geese and Sunsets—"Wowwww, Dad!"

How old were you when you first noticed a beautiful sunset, the gentle and graceful flight of geese, or the shadows on the walls of the Grand Canyon at dusk? When did you first marvel at the palette of fall trees, the snowcapped peaks, or the spray from the ocean hitting the shore? I can tell you one thing—it wasn't during your childhood.

Kids have a dense filter covering their eyes and a barricade in their brains that somehow let them wander through life without being awed, or even aware, of the natural beauty around them. Mountain lakes, galaxy-filled nighttime skies, wildflowers in bloom? Nope. Kids don't see the forest *or* the trees! Well, that's not entirely true. Kids do notice ants. And spiders.

The disconnect between adults hoping to imbue their kids with an appreciation for the wonders around them, and kids who seemingly couldn't care less, can be disconcerting for parents. Our kids developed the annoying (but admittedly very cute) custom of responding to our "Hey, isn't that waterfall gorgeous?" with "Wowwww, Dad," droned in an unimpressed and pseudo-bored cacophony. At least their response confirmed they were occasionally awake on our hikes in the national parks.

So what's a parent to do when your best efforts to make outdoor moments special with your kids are rewarded with a collective yawn? Expect it, accept it, and be comforted by two important truths: First, what makes your moments with your kids special is not the scenery, it's the company; and second, kids do absorb your enthusiasm and energy, even if they miss the bluebirds and the lily pads. They'll balk at hiking, but they'll remember that their moments in the woods were fun because they were with you, sleeping in a tent, roasting marshmallows, eating s'mores, and telling stories. They'll remember the big rocks that they thought were bears, the tree roots they thought were snakes, stopping at the drive-through for root beer floats, and being grossed out at the camper dump site. Yes, they'll ignore the full harvest moon, the rainbows, and the fossils and fault lines in the hillside rocks, but at least they won't be playing computer solitaire in their rooms. They'll be with you, in the fresh air, doing things you can feel good about.

And then, sometime in late adolescence or early adulthood, a wondrous awakening occurs. The fog in their brains clears, and they start to notice the beauty of the world around them without your having to narrate or nag.

That's when you show them the pictures to prove that they were down this trail before, with you.

Communication

Shareholder Meetings

If things are running smoothly in a household, families should be meeting all the time. Often those encounters don't involve everyone at once and are on the fly—in the car en route to school or errands; doing the microwave mambo before work; during bath time and bedtime rituals. Those fleeting meetings typically deal with immediate and practical issues, like who's driving whom where and when, whose turn is it in the bathtub, what time judo class is over today, and what we should do for dinner tonight.

The most important and recurrent meetings are during the one mealtime where everyone sits down together; those gatherings firmly anchor the family, sharing the happenings of the day, setting the plans for tomorrow, and dealing with the little issues that crop up all the time.

But periodically there are circumstances when formal "shareholder meetings" are necessary. In the corporate world, shareholders (those who hold a stake in the company) are called together to discuss the big things: earnings and dividends, mergers and acquisitions, advances in research and development, the election of new board members, etc. The business of being in a family is also serious and important enough to, on an as-needed basis, hold meetings that include everyone in the family, regardless of age. All the shareholders. This is the time for everyone to contribute, in their own way, on matters that affect the whole family or the family dynamic. Issues may include vacation planning, choice of schools, summer camp, family budgets, college decisions, buying a car, redecorating the house, or getting a pet. Of course, shareholder meetings are mandatory for the REALLY BIG ISSUES, like moving to a new city or changes in the family structure (marriage, divorce, remarriage, a new baby on the way, the death of a grandparent).

The issues at shareholder meetings must be carefully framed, in terms appropriate for your kids' ages. But even with the very youngest kids, major issues deserve a major meeting. The only way that shareholder meetings can serve their purposes is if everyone is given a chance to participate, because everyone holds a stake in the family. No opinion is unworthy; no suggestion is without merit; no concern is baseless. But to continue the corporate metaphor, parents are the CEOs, they run the shareholder meetings, and they make sure everyone has his or her fair say. Most important, the kids need to know from the outset of the meeting that the ultimate decisions regarding the big issues will be made by their parents. This is a forewarning to the kids that parents may decide something the kids disagree with, but it's also a relief for kids to know that the weight of big decisions is not on their shoulders. Kids can express their opinions freely, knowing that they will be heard but will not be responsible for the outcome.

Tell the kids that they are, indeed, the family shareholders and their voices matter. Tell them you will carefully consider everything they suggest, and that your mind is not made up yet. Tell them that you can be better parents when you know how your kids honestly feel about important family matters.

And, best of all, everything you tell them is true, which makes your family the most honest "corporation" in the world.

Photographic Memory

One of the harshest realizations for a parent is that young kids often forget those events that are the most memorable for parents. Of course, we hope our kids remember the "big picture"—that they are happy and loved, and that being our kids has been a good thing for them. But there's a way to help your kids with the "little pictures" as well: by actually showing them the little pictures as they grow up. Maintaining a real-time photo album, hard copy or digital, allows you to sit down with your kids at quiet times and show them how cute they were when they were littler, and how much they enjoyed that special trip to Grandma's or to Disneyland. Photo albums make great bedtime stories and help long car rides and plane trips go by faster. Home videos are another easy way to relive with your kids the fun moments of their younger days. Photos and videos give you an opportunity to tell your kids stories that they can uniquely relate to (because they are the lead characters!) and reinforce some of the happy memories they may have lost in the whirlwind that is childhood.

When they're older, it won't matter much if their recollections of childhood events are from the actual events or from your retelling of those events photographically. What will matter is that they know how they got to be who and where they are today, how much fun they had, and how much love and care went into the process. The bonus benefit is that the time you and your kids spend together revisiting the past through photos and videos will generate new moments of laughter and intimacy with your kids. And, those new moments themselves will become cherished memories.

Speaking Their Language

The world is shrinking. Every day brings us closer to the international community, yet Americans remain largely monolingual. Your kids may study a second language in school, but experience suggests that most school language programs fail to produce fluent speakers. This presents another marvelous opportunity for "double dipping," participating in a worthwhile activity with your kids that is equally beneficial and enjoyable for all of you.

For the price of an inexpensive computer "app" or set of CDs, you and your kids can learn a second language together. Hours in the kitchen, in the car, in doctor and dentist waiting rooms, and on airplanes can become a cultural and often comedic experience as all of you stumble over new words, experiment with new sentence structures, and cruelly mimic the faceless teacher's stiff voice.

The endpoints of this exercise are up to you. It may be just a summer's dalliance that everyone agrees has run its course by fall. Or it may lead to renting foreign-language movies, or English-language movies that are dubbed (or subtitled) in your new tongue. It may develop into a playgroup with kids for whom your new language is their first language. You may start to read books with your kids in your second language, or maybe you'll even travel together to a country where the language is spoken.

Like most undertakings with kids, the means can justify the ends, whatever the ends turn out to be. Learning, laughing, and sharing this new adventure together is all good, regardless of whether any of you ever *parlez, habla,* or *sprechen.*

Let "Ur" Fingers Do the Talking

Text messaging, Facebook, Twitter, Myspace, and kids' other e-distractions offer new avenues of communication between you and your kids if you are willing to learn to let your fingers do the talking. Much has been written about the potential dangers of online chat rooms, where kids can be stalked, swindled, and seduced—those are real dangers, and you and your digital-age kids should have a frank talk about those risks and come up with a family policy. Perhaps the safest way for you to protect your kids from online risks is to join those chats. If your kids let you "friend" them on Facebook, jump at the chance—but don't hold your breath; your kids probably won't welcome you as that kind of "friend." You will have to oversee the privacy features your kids choose on Facebook, as well as their friend list, but your family online policy will probably require something other than your direct participation in your kids' social-media chatter.

Which brings us to text messaging. As one who once wondered why anyone needed e-mail (I've since wised up), text messaging seemed like just another way of tracking me down and tying me up. Exactly! There is something magical about the immediacy and efficiency of texting that makes the same kids, who will never listen to their cell phone voicemail, answer texts on the very same cell phone. Kids tolerate texting from parents, maybe because it's not very disruptive, maybe because their friends don't have to know it's you on the other end, or maybe because it speaks your kids' language better than the other ways you try to communicate with them.

And what a blessing it is that kids tolerate your texting. The worry that our own parents' generation had about our whereabouts and goings-on is cured, at least partially, by texting your kids and asking, "Wer RU?", "Sup?", or "Wat's ur timing?" (Translation: "Where are you?", "What's up?", and "What's your timing?") When they answer, and whatever their answer is, you know enough for now. But in addition to the loose leash that text messaging puts on your kids, it connects you to them at times in the day that you otherwise wouldn't be connected. After big tests, before important games, during teen parties—you can touch base with your kids and, in addition to the actual text messages that pop up on their screens, you send them important encrypted messages: Their activities are important to you, and you are with them in spirit. Digital spirit.

Text them to be careful, what time you expect them home, where you'll pick them up. Let them know where you are and what you're doing between now and dinner; update them on your important meeting or speech. Complain ("My boss stinks"), brag ("They loved my presentation!"), coordinate ("Dinner after lacrosse practice?"). Set the tone for family texting as open, funny, and loving—and your kids will do the same. Send smiley faces or frowning faces. Learn the shorthand (LOL, BFF, TTYL, U2, K) and use it so your kids can tease you about your lame attempts to be cool. Texting hooks you up with your kids in real time, if only for abbreviated bursts of shorthand chat.

There is a very important additional motive to becoming regular text buddies with your kids: The habit carries over to college, where, as you'll read in Part 3 (the Epilogue), texting may be your main form of contact with your kids.

Long-Distance Connections

A generation ago, kids called home from college on Sundays because that's when the long-distance rates were cheaper. Grandparents living far from their children and grandchildren rarely saw or heard from them. Military personnel stationed far away stood in long lines for a turn to make a three-minute call to loved ones. Moving to another state or country meant writing letters and post-cards, or losing touch entirely with those who were close to you.

Welcome to the satellite and cable generation! While cell phones may have started the long-distance connectivity that we enjoy today, the technology has quickly moved beyond simply being able to dial up (punch in) anyone, anywhere, and anytime at a reasonable price. Now, Internet video "phone" service (e.g., Skype) allows you to bring grandchildren to the computer screens of their grandparents—entirely for free! You can welcome long-ago friends back into your lives and living rooms. You can conduct "face-to-face" business meetings online and reduce your work-related travel. Did I mention that this service is free?!!

Not only does Internet video phone service bring people back into your lives and let you stay in town for more business meetings, it also gives you more of what *No Regrets Parenting* is all about—quality moments with your kids. When they move out for college or jobs, you'll be able to continue to be a visible part of their lives. But beginning in the crib, and all the way through their growing-up years, time with your kids crowded in front of the computer-screen camera is an intimate, loving, and fun activity. They can show off for grandparents, joke with uncles and aunts, do magic tricks for their cousins, and stay connected to friends who moved away. Yes, Facebook, e-mailing, instant messaging, and texting also keep kids connected. But they do so without all the important social skills that come from face-to-face contact.

More important, from a parent's perspective, when your kids communicate by text or instant message or Facebook "friending," you're usually not part of that experience with them. But when your kids are on your lap or sitting next to you, talking to and seeing Grandma, they are sharing themselves not just with Grandma, but with you, too. Time together, you and your kids, putting on a little show and tell.

And what a godsend that is for Grandma!

Spirit and Soul

Charity Starts in the Home

There are always those who are less fortunate than you and your family. Those individuals offer your kids lessons in humility and opportunities for generosity. A multitude of foundations around the country have youth boards, kids appointed to help allocate a portion of the foundations' charitable resources. The kids on these boards research potentially worthy recipients of grants and donations. This is a win–win situation—teaching tomorrow's leaders about charity, as well as opening their eyes to the needy and less advantaged in their communities. The foundations' youth boards do terrific work, but there is no reason every family shouldn't have its own youth board at home. Except for the most destitute of situations, most people give some charity every year. They may write personal checks, give at the office, bring used clothes to a collection bin, or toss coins into a homeless person's hat on the street corner. But almost every family gives.

Giving is good. It's good for the heart and the soul, and it's good for your kids to see and experience. And, of course, it's good for the recipients of your generosity. Decide on the type and amount of charity you would like to give this year, and sit down with your kids to decide together how to distribute the money. Research worthy organizations, visit local missions or shelters, decide which groups use their donations in the best way to serve their populations— and do all of that with your kids. When your kids are younger, the "research" may simply be explaining a little to them about blindness or homelessness or cancer. As your kids get older, they can volunteer side by side with you at a soup kitchen, at an abused women's shelter, or with the Special Olympics. Take a charity walk together; before you go, gather sponsors who will contribute for every mile—and do that with your kids, too. When they're old enough, your kids can volunteer on their own at the local hospital. What better way to teach your kids gratitude for your family's many blessings? And what better way to "double dip" (see Part 1, "Staying Sane"), doing things with your kids that are enjoyable and fulfilling for all of you.

By including your kids in charitable acts and volunteering, you amplify the good deeds that those activities produce—you are teaching and role modeling for the next generation of givers.

Time spent together with your kids, for the benefit of others.

Keep the Faith

Sharing your belief system with your kids is a worthwhile and meaningful expression of quality time. You may or may not be observant of a particular faith, and you may or may not be a spiritual person. But whatever you are, it is you. And remember that in our re-defining of quality time, moments that allow your kids to better know you are precious and should be nurtured.

Sharing your beliefs with your kids will influence their beliefs just as everything you share about yourself with your kids influences them. You may want your children to accept the doctrines you were taught as a child because you continue to believe in them; or, perhaps as an adult you now question those concepts but still want your kids to have the same foundation you had growing up. You may have evolved away from your own religious upbringing and found a new and meaningful belief system. Or you may not have particular religious beliefs, which in and of itself can be an important insight for your kids into who you are.

Often discussing your beliefs with your kids allows you to better define those tenets for yourself, and may even renew convictions that have faded over the years. Kids are inquisitive; their questions will force you to find answers for yourself, as well as for them. Whatever aspirations you have for your kids' faith, the act of sharing yourself in this way is powerful and profound. It is also at the very heart of *No Regrets Parenting*, which holds that time spent with your kids benefits them and you, and is to be cherished.

While you are sharing your belief system with your kids, take the opportunity to teach them about other faiths. Understanding the world around them requires kids to understand what others hold true and how those principles affect behaviors. If your kids ask you about a friend's or classmate's religion or philosophy of life, spend time together in the library or searching the Internet for information and insight into the important foundations of people's lives. Use religious holidays, yours or others', as a starting point for discussions. Attend interfaith worship services to expose your kids to different philosophies of life.

In addition to your beliefs, share your values with your children. Religious faiths espouse strong value systems, hence bringing your child up in a particular faith will naturally expose him to the values of that faith. This book has subtly, and in some cases not so subtly, suggested certain values that I feel are important for kids to learn. But the most important values for your kids to learn are not those that I suggest or even those that are attendant with your religious beliefs—unless those values reflect you and what's important to you. It's your values that will be passed on to your kids because they absorb them by watching you live them. Your life should reflect the values you want your kids to inherit.

Which brings us back to *No Regrets Parenting*. When you are there for your kids, finding time for them throughout their childhood, they pattern their lives and the choices they make following the template you provide for them. Your beliefs and your values are at the core of who you are. Share them with your kids and, by doing so, you will be sharing yourself with your kids.

PART 3

Epilogue
College and Beyond

A Quick Review

*B*efore moving on to the subject of college, let's review your accomplishments to date. You have spent the past eighteen years conducting an intense college preparatory class. It began in the delivery room, perhaps even in the womb, when your baby first felt your love. As your child grew, she felt your love grow, as well, and she learned to love you back. At a certain very young age, your baby also began to observe your behavior; as she watched, she became more and more conscious of who you were, how you acted, and what you believed. Soon your little girl could ask questions, and she did, non-stop. And you diligently taught her, not only by your answers, but also by your patience and honesty. When you were wrong, you admitted it and apologized. Because you were there for her, practicing *No Regrets Parenting*, capturing the moments that would otherwise have been lost to "efficiency," she learned to trust you. And as she matured into her teen years, the trust that she learned from you paid off—you realized you could trust her, too.

All along, you set limits. From the first time you pulled up the crib railing to the curfew you enforced on your driving teens, you provided the structure and set the limits that every child needs. With this structure, and by your own role modeling, you taught your kids right from wrong. Yet, you never lost sight of their need to grow their independence, and you gave them space. When their bedroom doors were closed, you knocked. While never completely lowering your antennae, you kept a respectful distance when they were with friends. By balancing limits with liberty, you taught them respect—you for them, and they for you. And you gave your kids a road map for adult behavior.

Love, trust, and respect. Those are your accomplishments as a *No Regrets* parent.

Now comes the hard part. And the fun part. It's time to see how the prototype young adult you molded in your home functions on his own. How well does the mutual love, trust, and respect that you nurtured during his eighteen college preparatory years hold up under the pressures of college? And as for you, how do you negotiate a path that allows you to continue to be a part of his life without regressing into pre-college parenting patterns, reversing all that you and he accomplished to get him here? This is THE moment when he should be putting all you taught him into practice. You mustn't take that moment away from him, or from you.

Now it's time for you to grow up with your children.

Growing Up with Your Children

This final part of the book may, for some of you, feel like a distant mirage. If you still have young kids at home, picturing their college or work years may seem wildly premature. But much as you've started saving money for your kids' college educations, so you should also begin to think about building strategies for your relationships with your someday-soon-to-be college or workforce children. And if your kids are already on their way out the door, use these next chapters as a blueprint for maintaining the wonderful bonds you have worked so hard to create. You began building the fundamentals of these relationships while your kids were still in diapers; by the time they earned their driver's licenses, you were almost ready. Almost. Because nothing can quite prepare you for THE moment.

The previous chapters on principles and strategies of *No Regrets Parenting* help you capture the precious moments while your kids are young, anticipating THE moment. THE moment when you're standing at their new dorm rooms or apartments, or packing the car on your driveway, setting them "free" for college or their other young-adult pursuits. THE moment may be one you've been dreading, or one you've been eagerly anticipating; either way, it's likely to be a moment filled with immense pride, nostalgia, and perhaps melancholy. But if you've been successful in your *No Regrets Parenting*, it will not be a moment of remorse or disappointment.

But now that THE moment has arrived and your kids are moving into the next very exciting phase of their lives, it's time for you to grow up with them and move into this next very exciting phase of your life. The goal of turning scarce minutes into cherished moments now becomes more challenging than ever, and comes with a twist. As the nest empties and the complex choreography of having kids at home ebbs, you may find yourself with more time on your hands than you've been accustomed to for years. You're not rushing from work to catch their basketball game, or adjusting your morning schedule to drive car pool. But now it's your kids' minutes that are scarce—they have jam-packed class or work schedules, busy social lives, growing responsibilities.

Of course, nature helps you make this transition gradually—as your kids grow from infants, to toddlers, to "middle-age" children, to tweens, and finally to adolescents, they progressively and appropriately separate themselves from your schedule. You read in the earlier parts of this book about recognizing and welcoming those biological changes as new opportunities to share precious moments with your kids. You learned strategies for accommodating your kids' growth by reprogramming your time accordingly. The biggest change in your pre-college agenda with your kids undoubtedly occurred when they began driving on their own—your chauffeuring skill was one of the last tethers you had to your teens; when your kids no longer need a ride, the countdown to liftoff begins. It is likely that you spent more quality time in a week with your seven-year-old than in a year with your seventeen-year-old. That's both normal and good. It prepares both you and your seventeen-year-old for the following year.

But the "following year" has now arrived, and it's time to again reprogram your time accordingly. There are four keys to successfully making this next exciting transition in your relationship with your kids: preparation, communication, participation, and visitation. The following chapters are devoted to those principles—*No Regrets Parenting* for your kids' college and work years.

Preparation for Launch

The weeks between high school graduation and starting college are a whirlwind of logistical and practical to-do lists for you and your kids. Shopping for clothes, linens, and laptops; packing and shipping; booking transportation; farewell get-togethers with friends and family. Add to that your work and their summer job schedules, and you've got scant minutes before they leave. But make time for one additional and very important to-do list: the list you make to prepare your kids for what they should expect in college, and what you expect of them in college.

Don't assume that all systems are go just because you've been preparing them for college liftoff for eighteen years. Kids leave home at variable stages of readiness and maturity. It's unlikely, for example, that any high school graduate has had experience with a class schedule where some days don't start till noon, other days may have only two classes, and still others have nighttime lectures, labs, or study groups. It's doubtful that your kids' high school experiences adequately prepared them for dorm life, cafeteria dining choices, or sorority pledging. While it is unfortunately true that many kids in high school have seen friends drink or use drugs, and that sex among high schoolers is not rare, the level of all of those exposures may rise to a new logarithmic scale in college.

It's not enough to kiss your kids good-bye and whisper in their ear, "Use your head; we trust you to do what's right; we respect your choices; we love you." Schedule a meeting with your freshman-to-be.

Do it formally, sitting down, with a cup of tea or a Coke, and with the "College Launch List." This is your compilation of all the things you can think of to tell them before they leave, no matter how many times you've told them the same things over the past eighteen years.*

Talk about uncomfortable subjects; make them squirm a little (*"Mommmm!* C'mon, I know all that!") or a lot. Of course, they won't remember every word you say about dormitory fire escapes or which foods are healthy or setting two alarm clocks on test mornings, but they will remember the biggies—maybe because those are the ones that make them squirm the most. This is the ultimate in quality time with your child—it is your graduation speech to them as you transition from being the parent of a child to being the parent of a young adult.

More than ever, you now need to carve out special moments with your child from the scarce minutes of his liftoff summer. Set aside at least a couple hours, maybe in two sittings, and cover every topic on your list until you feel comfortable that he's heard what he needs to hear from you. Make sure it's not a one-way conversation. Ask him if he understands what you're saying and why you're saying it. Tell him about your own experiences that color your perspective, and about news stories you've read or anecdotes you've heard that scare you about college life. This is one of the most important parenting opportunities you will have for a long time. It becomes much harder to be intimately involved in your kids' lives once they are out the door (but, as you'll read in the upcoming chapters, not impossible!). By the time they leave, you should have *No Regrets* that you missed this chance for parting words and for imparting wisdom.

Then, after you've gone through every item on your list, it's time to give your child a hug and a kiss, and whisper in his ear, "Use your head; we trust you to do what's right; we respect your choices; we love you."

---

* See the Appendix at the end of the book for a sample "College Launch List," a template of topics to get you started. Tailor the list to your child; delete those items that aren't necessary to discuss, and add others that are.

Campus Communication

A generation ago, kids called home from college on Sunday evenings because that's when exorbitant long-distance phone rates were a little cheaper. Today, parents of college kids have almost unfettered access to their new frosh: cell phones, text messaging, instant messaging, Facebook, Twitter, video Internet calling, etc. Of course, that's assuming you know how to use any of those technologies, but even if it's "just" cell phone communication, you may be shocked to find that your kids are more accessible to you on campus than they were in high school! That's a privilege that needs to be handled responsibly if you want to make sure they call frequently and answer when you call.

In addition to being more accessible, your college kids may actually need you more now than in high school. Sounds strange, I know, since college is their inaugural of independence. But college can also be very stressful, especially during freshman year. Homesickness is universal, although not every kid will admit to it. And the new academic and social challenges facing a first-year college student can be overwhelming. During high school, home provided subconscious security and stability that gave your kids the chance to develop self-confidence and early independence. As high school seniors, they were on top of their game. Now, in college, their confidence may be shaky and they may not be feeling too comfortable with their newfound autonomy.

Your timely communication with them during their college lives can ease them through this transition without making them feel like you are hovering or meddling. Here are some methods and moments for staying in touch:

WALKING TO CLASS—In ranch and rodeo parlance, the job of the "cutting horse" is to separate one cow from the herd. Much of your kids' time during their first year of college is spent in herds—groups of friends in the dorm, dining halls, libraries. Cutting your calf from his herd long enough for a real conversation is nearly impossible; when he's with his friends, you're intruding. But there are solo moments in your college student's life. Thanks to the quirkiness of class schedules, diversity of majors, and distances between buildings, your child's walk to and from classes is often alone, and an ideal time for a quick burst of "Hi, Mom, how's it going?" But the calls have to come from them; otherwise you'll roll over into voice mail that never gets listened to. If you're lucky, your kids will think of calling you en route to classes on their own because it's a practical solution—they won't have to squeeze in a call to you later in the day, and they are less likely to be interrupted from what they're doing by your calls to them. If they don't think of it on their own, drop a hint—"I never know the right time to call that won't disturb you in class or studying, so why don't you call me when you have ten minutes between classes?" That sends two important messages: CALL ME MORE OFTEN and MAKE SURE YOU GO TO CLASSES.

TEXT ART—After spending most of your kids' middle school and high school years tolerating your kids' text messaging as a necessary evil with few redeeming qualities (one of which was, admittedly, your ability to send them messages and often even get a response), you should become a devoted text artist the minute they leave for college. I can't explain why college kids won't answer their phones when you call, don't check their voice mail, and never open your e-mail—yet do answer your texts. It's probably because texting has become mindless—they don't even realize they're doing it! They can receive and respond to texts in microseconds, blindly, without looking at the keyboard or screen. Remember how you cringed when you sensed their fingers moving stealthily under the kitchen table at dinner? Kids can walk, talk, *and* chew gum while texting.

But what a relief it is for a parent who hasn't heard from a college kid for a few days to be able to text "Doin ok?" and get back a "Ya!" Or on your kids' more communicative days, "Ya U?" Texting is practically noninvasive. Your kids don't mind getting your texts, they answer them, and then they keep doing what they're doing without missing a beat. So, now it's up to you, if you haven't already jumped in with both feet while they were in middle school or high school, to learn the art of the brief college questions: "Test go ok?" or "Feeling better?" The art of the brief request: "Call ltr 4 quick ??'" Or "Check ur mail; sent $." Or "Mom's b-day call her." And the art of the brief endearment: "Luv U!" or "XOXOXO!" or "Good luck today!" And fully expect to hear back in kind: "K," "U2," or "Thx."

FACEBOOK—Talk about a "killer app"! In the old days (before 2004), friends from summer camp, middle school, high school, the neighborhood, and the soccer team gradually lost track of one another as those phases of life passed. Not everyone, of course. The closest friends stayed in touch with old-fashioned tools like telephones and e-mail—or, amazing as it may seem today, actual face-to-face contact. Today, nobody loses touch with anyone—including the people you'd like to lose touch with. The Facebook phenomenon has reinvented the way we communicate. It is a near certainty that if your kids are old enough to hunt and peck on a keyboard, they have Facebook "walls." When your kids were younger, you probably oversaw the privacy features and "friends" they chose. Now that they are in college, you have to surrender that oversight and hope your kids remember the rules of online safety that you taught them before they left home. And frankly, the stuff they see and hear on Facebook is nothing compared with what they see and hear at their first frat party.

Which brings us to your asking your kids to be their Facebook "friend," something they were highly unlikely to agree to when they were at home. Why should your kids "friend" you now when they didn't in high school? Because, you'll argue, it lets you be a part of their lives even though they are many miles away. A flagrant appeal to their consciences and sensibilities, yes, but you have leverage to offer. The more you can see of their friends, parties, and musings on Facebook, the less you'll pry in person or by phone. I agree, that's not a lot of leverage, but it's worth a try. And don't Facebook "stalk" your kids, prying into their friends' lives or activities. As with all college communication, be careful not to abuse the privilege of being a part of your kids' lives.

TWITTER—Follow your kids on Twitter and have them follow you. If you don't know what that means, you're in good company. Google it.

CARE PACKAGES—It sounds quaint, but you can still communicate with your kids by mail. The best snail-mail deliveries include "care packages" from home: baked treats, gag items, decorations for their room, news clippings with updates from their hometown or high school. Send care packages for birthdays, holidays, and for no special reason at all. Make sure you text them to tell them they have mail. Real mail. Otherwise they'll never check their mailboxes.

The tone of your communications with your college kids, by whatever medium you converse in, must be different than the tone you used with high schoolers. College coincides with legal emancipation—although your eighteen- to twenty-two-year-olds may still act like kids at times, they are no longer minors in the eyes of the law. It is now time for them to no longer be minors in your eyes, either. Talk to them like adults—at least like young adults. Be less managing, less monitoring, less disciplining, and less demanding. And be more deferential to their judgment, more flexible in your expectations, more respectful of their privacy, and more appreciative of how grown up they've become.

Postgraduate Participation

After mastering the art of integrating yourself into your kids' calendars and activities from preschool through twelfth grade, there is no reason to stop just because they are graduating from high school and starting college. But you must protect your young-adult kids from feeling like they're still in middle school.

So, how do you find the right balance for participating in your kids' college experience without regressing? It all goes back to the love, trust, and respect you nurtured in their pre-college years. Recall from Part 1 of this book that throughout their childhoods, you are not only your kids' parent, you're also their best friend. Now is the time to stifle, or at least camouflage, some of your parental urges and allow your best friend qualities to blossom. Ask questions her roommate might ask. Ask which classes she plans to take; write down her schedule so you'll know what she's studying (and when not to disturb her). Ask about her extracurricular activities: dorm life, intramural sports, clubs. Learn her friends' names—maybe she'll even let you see their pictures on Facebook (see the previous chapter). Find out how far she has to walk to the library and which library she likes best. Know when she has important meetings with her adviser. Help her think through her options for picking majors and minors, joining sororities, spring breaks, and summer jobs.

BUT HERE'S THE IMPORTANT PART: Don't do it all at once, and don't do it in parent mode. Get used to microbursts of communication with your college kids (see the previous chapter); learn to ask what you need to learn in a minute or two, because that's how much time you have before one of their roommates or classmates walks by and you hear "Gotta go, Mom, love you." Avoid the temptation to pack too much information gathering into the call, forgetting to just chat about the hometown football team, a great movie you saw, or how uncomfortable Dad looked in the rented tux at the cousin's wedding last night.

From now on, be friend first, parent second. At least that's the way your college kids should perceive it. If you're clever about it, you'll always be parent first, no matter how old your kids are—but they should become less aware of your parenting and more aware of how wise and trusted a friend you have become. This is a grown-up version of the "subliminal togetherness" strategy described in Part 1 of this book.

Using the examples from above, here's how the answers to the "best friend" questions you've asked let you participate in your college kids' lives without being too intrusive:

CLASSES—Make sure she signs up for enough, but not too many hours; she should be busy, but not overwhelmed. It's okay to take a lighter freshman load; she can make up the credits during the next year when she's more settled in school. Ask her if you can log onto the course catalog from home and read about the classes so you'll know what she's learning. Maybe one of the classes she's thinking about sounds bad or boring. Talk about it with her—as a friend, not as a parent. The decision is still hers. Or if you find something that looks great in the catalog, ask if she's heard about that class or thought about adding it for this semester or next. During finals, she may welcome your advice on how to juggle all the tests and papers—time management is not a required high school course, and many kids go to college with suboptimal juggling skills.

EXTRACURRICULAR ACTIVITIES AND FRIENDS—Use your trained parent ears to screen for potential trouble: too many parties, friends who party too hard, road trips she shouldn't be taking. And while that conversation starts out as friend to friend, a "what's happening in your life" type of chat, if your radar senses trouble, shift into parent mode and parent. As astonishing as it may seem, your college kids still need structure and want to hear your advice—you may have less control over whether they follow the advice you give, but it's still your job to give it. And although they may groan, *"Daaaaad . . . !!!"* when you slip from best friend into parent mode, if you've practiced *No Regrets Parenting* before they left home, they won't be surprised—they still expect you to be their guidepost in this new adventure.

WALK TO THE LIBRARY—Her answer lets you remind her that campuses can be unsafe and that walking to and from the library, or anywhere else, at night should always be with a friend.

ADVISER MEETINGS—This helps you participate in the advising process—understanding what he's hearing from his adviser lets you provide your own feedback and ask your own questions that he can reframe as his. It also lets you judge whether the advising process is adequate and whether he needs to find better counsel.

MAJORS AND MINORS, SORORITIES, SPRING BREAKS, AND SUMMER JOBS—Asking these questions assures your child that you are always there for the big branch points in her life. And you assure yourself that she is on target in her maturation toward being ready to make the even bigger life decisions that will come along.

Kids in college do not fly on their own immediately—they still need you in their lives. Participation in your kids' campus lives looks different than when they were at home. But it is vitally important participation, nonetheless. Be their friend and confidant—those are hard-won accomplishments that you earned in their first eighteen years. Be their parent, but be sure to give them enough independence that they feel the college difference. That's a hard-won accomplishment they earned.

Parenting becomes more nuanced and subtle when your kids are in college. Embrace that challenge. It requires a fresh mentality, shifting from enabling and enforcing to entrusting and enfranchising.

And, of course, enriching the university with your tuition dollars, very tangible evidence of your participation in your college kids' lives.

Visitation Rights (and Wrongs)

If you are fortunate and your kids attend college within "laundry distance" (i.e., they can get home with dirty laundry on weekends), seeing your college kids is not that dramatically different from high school. If they live at home while attending a city or community college, it's exactly like high school. Although your local college students have wildly different schedules than you, you still have the luxury of the occasional dinner together, shared birthday celebrations, going to the big game as a family, and, of course, coordinating laundry hours. Take full advantage of their proximity without being invasive or intrusive—recognize that they have earned the privacy and independence rights of young adults even though they may have chosen, or finances may have required them, to be closer to home. Invite them to join you for family events, but don't demand their participation. Lower your expectations for how much time you will have together, be appreciative for that time, and be sensitive to their feelings about being close by—some kids are very comfortable with it and even prefer to be close; others are embarrassed that Mom and Dad are still hanging around them in college. Don't be hurt if your kids are in the latter category—living close to home after high school graduation, at the precise time that their independence biology is peaking, may be a necessary compromise but can be difficult for some kids. It's not you they are rejecting, but rather their dependency on you—and that's okay.

In contrast to laundry distance, if your kids move to "frequent-flier distance" for college, you may have a unique opportunity to develop a second career as a travel agent and play airline roulette with fares and flight schedules. When your kids are across the country, seeing them in person may become a once- or twice-a-year event if you're not innovative in planning their visits home and your visits to them. Yes, there's the almost miraculous (and free) video Internet phone service to help bridge the time and make sure your kids are eating and shaving (I've even used Internet video phone to decide if our freshman's basketball laceration needed stitches! "Hold your forehead a little closer to the camera . . ."). But for *No Regrets* parents like yourselves who have become accustomed to intimate involvement in your kids' lives for the past eighteen years, in-person visits will be essential to maintaining your sanity. And hopefully after growing up in a *No Regrets Parenting* home, your kids will feel the same.

Visits with your faraway college kids fall into two categories: big events and cameo appearances. The big events include major holidays, major college occasions (freshman orientation and move-in week, Parents' Weekend, graduation), and school vacations. Major holidays usually mean your kids are traveling home; major college occasions mean you are traveling to college; and school vacations can be either or both. Sounds daunting, but doing this right will make the difference between a painful, abrupt separation and a fulfilling, gradual mutual growth for you and your kids. Keeping your family together for the big events requires advance planning and a willingness to prioritize your time and forgo other expenses.

Planning is the easy part. Major college occasions are posted on the school's Web site well ahead of the start of the school year. Enter all of those dates for the entire college year into your master calendar at home, much as you did for your kids' after-school activities when they were little. That way, you'll RSVP "no" when you're invited to a wedding the same weekend as Parents' Weekend. You'll also know exactly when their final exam periods are over, and when fall, winter, spring, and summer breaks start and end. That allows you to schedule your work vacations during their vacations.

Sharing big events with your college kids requires the same time and money prioritization skills you honed when they were home. This goes back to the fundamental question I asked in the Introduction of this book: Who are you? By now, as you've reached the Epilogue, I know the answer to that. You are a parent first; otherwise you wouldn't have read this far. And the priorities in your life that guided you through the first eighteen years with your child will continue to guide you. If you and your spouse need a getaway for just the two of you, you won't schedule it during your kids' winter college break any more than you would have when they were in middle school. As much as possible, you'll tweak your work schedule to accommodate the college calendar. Family time is still whenever you can grab it and is still about turning scarce minutes into cherished moments. Setting priorities with money hasn't changed, either. To share the time off that colleges give your kids, you will probably have to forgo a new car or remodeling the house for a few years. But you're used to that, too.

Cameo appearances are the other category of visitations with your college kids. If you're lucky, there will be occasional, fluky opportunities that come up during which you can sneak in a trip to see your kids. A business trip to a big city that's located close enough for a train ride up to campus (business in New York followed by a comfortable three-hour commuter ride to Boston) to take your daughter out to dinner. A vacation with your spouse that can be routed through a connecting city for an overnight visit with your son. Take advantage of a three-day weekend for a long drive and a short visit with your child—a road-trip getaway for you, and a quick fix of family time for all of you before his classes (and your work) start again on Tuesday morning. And then there's the midway option. If you're in California and your son is in Virginia, Chicago is midway. There may be times when flights are inexpensive enough, and/or everyone is missing each other so much, that a long weekend can mean a two-hour flight for you and for your daughter to meet for a couple days in a neutral but fun place. Cameo appearances are wonderful for mental health, and for bridging the time between vacations.

See your college kids as often as you can. I don't want to freak you out completely, but your time together will become even scarcer when they're married and have their own families. Unless they move back home with you . . . but that's a different book entirely.

CONGRATULATIONS!

*Y*ou've done it! They're in college or out in the world!

You have raised wonderful children who love their parents and know their parents. You turned countless childhood minutes, hours, days, and weeks that would have otherwise been lost in the name of expediency into special moments that you'll cherish forever. You were there with them every chance you had, and you created chances to be with them that you never imagined you could.

And as reward for your commitment, passion, and love, you can now pass by their empty bedrooms, feeling fond nostalgia and missing them terribly. But what a blessing it is to feel *No Regrets*!

The days were long, the years were short, and the time you had with them was then. But you made the time and you took the time.

Now it's your time. You earned it.

Appendix

The College
Launch List

ere's a template list to get you started for the important, formal meeting with your high school grad before college liftoff. I've alphabetized these items because only you can determine which should be at the top of your list. Tailor the list to your child; delete items that aren't necessary to discuss, and add others that are. Each topic on the list is written in your voice, as if you were saying it to your son or daughter. Note that all entries are "Twitter" length. If you don't know what that means, don't worry about it, because these items are not meant to be "tweeted" verbatim to your kids. They are meant to be prompts for you that lead to real two-way discussions about each topic.

ACTIVITIES/EXTRACURRICULAR—balance carefully with schoolwork; school is your priority.

ADVISERS—meet with them early and often; they can help pick classes and majors.

ALARM CLOCK—get to class on time; set two alarms on test days.

ASSIGNMENT BOOK/CALENDAR—record every assignment and meeting.

BOOKS—buy used if not too marked up; save money when you can.

CALL HOME—whenever you have a few minutes just to catch up; call your siblings often.

CAMERA—take pictures of your big moments; download and share some with us.

CIGARETTES—don't start; many lifelong smoking habits start in college.

CLOTHES/LAUNDRY—once a week is a good routine.

COMPUTER—lock up your laptop; these are stolen a lot.

COMPUTER REPAIR—you will need it at some point; find the office before you need it.

CULTURE—college is about more than classes; go to programs out of your comfort zone.

CUTTING CLASS—don't, even if the professor is boring; don't be late to class, either.

DIGITAL DISTRACTIONS—turn off Facebook, video games, YouTube until schoolwork is done.

DIVERSITY—be friends with people from as many different backgrounds as possible.

DRINKING—you know the drill, but I have to tell you again because it's important.

DRINKING 2—never walk away from your drink; if you do, don't drink it—get a new one.

DRUGS—you know the drill, but I have to tell you again; there is no "safe" drug.

EXERCISE—at least three times a week, for physical and mental health.

FIRE HAZARDS/FIRE ESCAPES/FIRE EXTINGUISHERS—find them on day one.

FOOD/MEAL PLAN—foods that were healthy at home are still healthy.

"FRESHMAN FIFTEEN"—avoid the weight gain from poor food choices and lack of exercise.

FRIENDS—pick them carefully; avoid people who are trouble—you know who they are.

GRADES—good grades make us proud; bad grades make us worry; work hard.

HAIRCUTS/SHAVING—you only get one chance to make a first impression.

HEALTH—sleep enough, eat right, exercise, wash your hands frequently.

HEALTH CLINIC—be comfortable getting checked out if you're worried.

HOMESICK—it happens to everyone; call home, Skype with us, let us help.

HOMEWORK HELP—use professors' office hours; there are also tutors for everything.

LECTURE HALLS—sit in front to stay awake and alert; don't Web surf during lectures.

LECTURE NOTES—take good notes to help you stay awake and alert, and to study later.

MAIL—we'll be sending surprise care packages, so check your mail often.

MAJOR AND MINOR—let us help you decide your college curriculum.

MEDICINE—don't share your medicine with others or take anyone else's.

MONEY—college is expensive; make wise choices; cut corners.

MOOD—be sensitive to your mood; if you're feeling depressed or sad, tell us right away.

MP3 PLAYER—keep it under watch; these are stolen a lot.

OPEN-MINDEDNESS—try new things (safe new things).

ORGANIZE—your desk, your room, your clothes drawers; no one's picking up after you.

PHONE—keep it under watch; these are stolen a lot.

PLAGIARISM/CHEATING—quickest way out of college; don't even glance around during tests.

POKER—not for money; college is expensive.

POLITICS—campus is rife with political activity and organizations; learn from them.

RICH KIDS/POOR KIDS—befriend people from diverse socioeconomic backgrounds.

SECURITY/SAFETY—lock your dorm door when you're out; don't walk alone at night.

SEX—you know the drill, but I have to tell you again because it's important.

SHOPPING—college is expensive, so make smart choices.

SLEEP—you need at least eight hours a night to learn effectively and stay healthy.

SPORTS—intramurals are great ways to meet people and get exercise.

STUDYING—this is why you're in college; everything else is a bonus.

TESTS/FINALS—college tests are going to be hard; allow plenty of time to prepare.

TIME OFF—sometimes a semester off can help if you're struggling; tell us and let's talk.

TRAVEL/ROAD TRIPS—we need to know about any off-campus travel you are planning.

VACATIONS—it's not too early to start thinking about how you'd like to spend breaks.

VISITS—we will be there as often as we can; if you need us urgently, tell us right away.

WEATHER—dress for the weather; cold and gray can be depressing; tell us if you are sad.

*D*r. Harley Rotbart has been a pediatric specialist for the past thirty years and is professor and vice chairman of pediatrics at the University of Colorado School of Medicine and Children's Hospital Colorado. He is a nationally recognized parenting expert, speaker, and educator, and is the author of more than 175 medical and scientific publications and two previous books for parents. Dr. Rotbart and his wife practice *No Regrets Parenting* with their three children in Denver, Colorado.

CPSIA information can be obtained
at www.ICGtesting.com
Printed in the USA
LVOW07*1442260417

532270LV00007B/122/P